CW01425527

Microsoft Dynamics NAV Administration

A quick guide to install, configure, deploy, and administer Dynamics NAV with ease

Sharan Oberoi

Amit Sachdev

[PACKT] PUBLISHING enterprise

professional expertise distilled

BIRMINGHAM - MUMBAI

Microsoft Dynamics NAV Administration

Copyright © 2010 Packt Publishing

All rights reserved. No part of this book may be reproduced, stored in a retrieval system, or transmitted in any form or by any means, without the prior written permission of the publisher, except in the case of brief quotations embedded in critical articles or reviews.

Every effort has been made in the preparation of this book to ensure the accuracy of the information presented. However, the information contained in this book is sold without warranty, either express or implied. Neither the authors, Packt Publishing, nor its dealers or distributors will be held liable for any damages caused or alleged to be caused directly or indirectly by this book.

Packt Publishing has endeavored to provide trademark information about all the companies and products mentioned in this book by the appropriate use of capitals. However, Packt Publishing cannot guarantee the accuracy of this information.

First published: September 2010

Production Reference: 1170910

Published by Packt Publishing Ltd.
32 Lincoln Road
Olton
Birmingham, B27 6PA, UK.

ISBN 978-1-847198-76-1

www.packtpub.com

Cover Image by Sandeep Babu (sandyjb@gmail.com)

Credits

Authors
Sharan Oberoi
Amit Sachdev

Reviewers
Dhan Raj Bansal
Tony Hemy

Acquisition Editor
Sarah Cullington

Development Editor
Reshma Sundaresan

Technical Editors
Gaurav Datar
Manjeet Kaur Saini

Copy Editors
Janki Mathuria
Sanchari Mukherjee

Editorial Team Leader
Gagandeep Singh

Project Team Leader
Ashwin Shetty

Indexer
Monica Ajmera Mehta

Proofreader
Sandra Hopper

Production Coordinators
Arvindkumar Gupta
Kruthika Bangera

Cover Work
Arvindkumar Gupta

Foreword

The Microsoft acquisition of Navision in 2002 changed this world-class ERP solution forever. Microsoft's deep R&D and extensive partner network fueled NAV into the fastest growing mid-market ERP globally. Hallmarks of Navision are its ease of installation, configuration, and use. Its strong architecture, layered development platform, and user-friendly interface enables quick ROI and high end-user adoption. From simple origins, NAV has grown into a fully scalable, robust application with strong positioning among the top-tier ERP products. The recent release of the RoleTailored client enables step-level changes in user adoption and productivity. More and more international businesses are adopting NAV, either as a hub and spoke model, or as an enterprise ERP application.

This book highlights some key areas of Dynamics NAV and the corresponding integration of other Microsoft technology. The book will appeal to beginners, users, and partners alike.

Dave Miller – General Manager, Microsoft Canada (MBS)

About Dave Miller

Dave Miller is the GM of MBS Canada. His team is responsible for driving the growth of the ERP and CRM businesses.

Dave has been in the IT industry for 23 years. His career has spanned services, outsourcing, infrastructure, and software. Dave has held positions of increasing responsibility with leading IT firms including Xerox, EMC, and most recently SAP, where he was Regional VP for Central Canada.

Dave holds an Honors Commerce degree from Laurentian University and a Bachelor of Science Degree in Computer Science from Brock University.

About the Authors

Sharan Oberoi is a seasoned Microsoft Dynamics professional and has more than 11 years of experience working as an architect, consultant, and business leader for Microsoft Dynamics products. He works for Tectura in an advisory role.

He has helped various organizations with large-scale, global, successful implementations of Microsoft Dynamics NAV. Sharan has also built and grown high-performing, culturally diversified, and geographically dispersed consulting teams. At the start of his Microsoft Dynamics career, Sharan was an instrumental startup team member for Microsoft Dynamics NAV (Navision) in India. He led a small team to localize and release Microsoft Dynamics NAV in India and subsequently evangelize Microsoft Dynamics NAV across the newly established partner channel in India.

Sharan worked as a consultant for a few US-end clients before moving to New Zealand. He gained his Big 4 consulting experience while working for Ernst & Young in New Zealand for a few years. In 2007, he moved to Vancouver, Canada with his family and started working as a team leader for Tectura. While at Tectura, Sharan has handled diverse roles and has been involved in various product teams and global clients, with complex, high-risk product implementations and application rollouts.

Having worked for organizations such as Tectura, Ernst & Young, and Navision (now Microsoft), Sharan has lived and worked in a dozen or more countries, touching almost every continent. He has worked with clients from diverse industries including ports, financial services, agri businesses, energy and power generation, shipping, and so on.

I believe my Thanks section would go longer than my own profile. I've taken so much from so many people in terms of love, support, knowledge, experience, and so on, that it would be unfair to miss any of them.

I would like to thank my wife Gurvinder for her unconditional support in this project. While I was busy toiling away for the last few months to write this book, she's been busy juggling her own work, taking care of our two beautiful kids, and helping me write this book. I hope I am able to compensate the time I stole from her quota.

Big thanks to my Dad, Mom, and Sister for believing in me and providing me with a rock-solid support and value system to live an honest and positive life, full of love, and giving me the confidence to always take the right path.

Thanks to all my friends and family who have been with us for so many years and to those who have supported me throughout the writing of this book.

Thanks a lot to my dear friend and coauthor of this book, Amit Sachdev, for his endurance, support, and knowledge for finishing this book.

I would like to express my sincere gratitude to Terry Petrzelka, Lisa Mathias, Vince Castiglione, Chris Harte, Chuck Famula, Kathy Nohr, Naeem Shafi, Tara, and Michael Hamby from Tectura, Claus Hamann from the ex Ernst & Young NAV team and Harmeet Singh from Microsoft for their encouragement and support during the writing of this book and otherwise.

I cannot thank enough, the *late* Mr. Yash Nagpal for keeping faith in my abilities and giving me some of the most important opportunities in the early years of my career.

For the many nights that I have not been able to tuck you both into bed and for the long winter evenings that I have not been able to play with you, while I was finishing up this book—this work is dedicated to the two precious jewels of my life Kudrat and Nimar.

Amit Sachdev works as a Technology Advisor for Dynamics products and the lead for SureStep methodology programs at Microsoft Canada. He is responsible for "Dynamics" product awareness, strategic engagement with Microsoft partners, building successful Dynamics practices, and ensuring the use of best principles for partners around delivery and implementation methodologies.

Amit has diverse professional experience, and in the past has worked in various capacities including advisory consulting, management, designing, and implementing business solutions in many countries, spanning across various industries and market segments.

He holds an Engineering degree in Electronics and various awards and certifications in both Microsoft and non-Microsoft technologies. Apart from his eminence as a seasoned "Dynamics" professional, Amit has also been instrumental in providing strategic direction to various startups and sits on the board and advisory panels of various non IT and IT-related companies.

I want to thank everyone who graciously agreed to help me in completing this book. I wouldn't have been successful without the support from my colleagues, my team, family, and friends who've always been there for me.

Although my list would be endless, I would particularly like to cite (in alphabetical order), Al Fournier, Brad Pawlak, Dan Brown, Dave Miller, Flemming Klaussen, Harmeet Singh, John MacDonald, Joyce Lafleur, Monica Sarna, Morris Mele, Raouf Kishk, and Vishal Rajput for their endless help and motivation.

I would be remiss if I did not convey my special gratitude to my friend and ex-colleague, Martin Beechener, Sharan Oberoi (the co-author of this book), and Tony Hemy (reviewer of this book) for their contribution, knowledge, and continuous support.

Last, but not least, my special thanks to my parents, my wife, my sister, and my lovely son, who have always believed in my abilities and provided me with all the love and happiness in life.

About the Reviewers

Dhan Raj Bansal graduated in Electronics & Instrumentation Engineering from Kurukshetra University. After scoring All India Rank 6 in the national-level entrance test called GATE (Graduate Aptitude Test in Engineering) in 2003, he got through in prestigious Indian Institute of Science, Bangalore (India) in M.Tech (Instrumentation Engineering). In 2005, he started his professional career as Navision Technical Consultant with PwC, India.

Currently Dhan Raj works as a Freelance NAV Developer and Business Analyst. He has worked for clients in the US, UK, Denmark, Australia, Dubai, Nigeria, and India.

Dhan Raj is an active member of the online communities for NAV, such as `dynamicsuser.net`, `mibuso.com`, and the online forums managed by Microsoft. For his contributions to these online communities, he received the Microsoft Most Valuable Professional (MVP) Award in July 2010. The MVP Award is given out by Microsoft to independent members of technology communities around the world, and recognizes people that share their knowledge with other members of the community.

Dhan Raj lives with his family in Gurgaon, India. He loves mathematics and solving puzzles.

Tony Hemy started working with Navision Financials straight out of secondary school in 1998 in Southampton, England.

In the years since, he has travelled the world developing and deploys Dynamics NAV in three Microsoft regions (North America, Asia Pacific and Europe, Middle East and Africa) and over a vast variety of industries.

Tony spent six years as a reserve soldier in the UK, the only break in his 12-year NAV career coming as a six-month United Nations peacekeeping tour in Cyprus with the British Army's Royal Regiment of Artillery.

Currently living in Vancouver, Canada as the Senior NAV Consultant at The RSC Group, Tony's work includes designing with Dynamics NAV code, as well as visioning and consulting.

Outside of work Tony enjoys mountaineering and rock climbing.

Table of Contents

Preface

Microsoft Dynamics NAV is an Enterprise Resource Planning (ERP) software product that integrates financial, manufacturing, supply chain management, sales and marketing, project management, human resources, and services management information from across your organization, into a centralized database. It can take hours to browse through documentation and references available online to learn how to install, configure, deploy and administer Dynamics NAV. This book aims to offer quickstart information in one place.

You will be amazed to find out how easily you can administer Dynamics NAV using this quick step-by-step guide. This book also has recommendations for software and hardware requirements, including operating system considerations and hardware considerations for administering Dynamics NAV to your advantage. It covers some advanced functions to set up periodic activities, common batch jobs, and create object files. It will also guide you to secure your database by creating backups and improve performance with practical examples.

What this book covers

Chapter 1, Setting up the Environment for Dynamics NAV, as the name suggests, is all about how we can set up the environment for Dynamics NAV, what the prerequisites are, among other things.

Chapter 2, Installing Dynamics NAV, discusses 5.0 SP1 Dynamics NAV C/SIDE client installations, followed by installation of a C/SIDE database server. It also walks us through the process of installing the Dynamics NAV 2009 RoleTailored client and also the Dynamics NAV server.

Chapter 3, Integrating Dynamics NAV with the Microsoft Platform, shows how Dynamics NAV is integrated with the rest of the Microsoft Stack, including SharePoint and other Office applications.

Chapter 4, Securing Dynamics NAV Applications, talks about security, roles, permissions, and other related topics for the Dynamics NAV application.

Chapter 5, Backing up and Restoring a Dynamics NAV Database, helps us create a backup and restore it using the Dynamics NAV client. It also looks at how to handle error messages encountered while restoring.

Chapter 6, Performance Tuning, is all about configuring a SQL Server database for Microsoft Dynamics NAV by defining database and transaction log files, configuring RAID 10, and defining rules using collations. It also looks into fine-tuning the performance of the database for Dynamics NAV by using Sum Index Flow Technology, and by accessing and modifying the properties of the indexes. Finally, the chapter also discusses identifying and troubleshooting performance issues by updating the statistics and using the tools available in SQL Resource Kit.

Chapter 7, Setting up Periodic Activities, Stylesheets, and Rapid Implementation Methodology, starts with how to set up recurring jobs, which can be run automatically at a preset time and a set frequency. It then speaks about the functional aspect and some of the most common batch jobs that are required in business. The final part talks about rapid implementation in NAV.

Chapter 8, Updating Objects and Virtualization with Dynamics NAV, speaks about what virtualization is, its types, and advantages. It then helps us understand how Dynamics NAV is supported in virtualization.

Chapter 9, Business Intelligence, starts with what Business Intelligence is, its categories, and product scenarios for each category. It then moves to the inherent BI capabilities in Dynamics NAV. Finally, it walks us through steps for designing reports in NAV 2009 and testing them.

Who this book is for

If you want to get started in administering Dynamics NAV, this book is for you. Readers need not have any previous experience with Dynamics NAV.

Conventions

In this book, you will find a number of styles of text that distinguish between different kinds of information. Here are some examples of these styles, and an explanation of their meaning.

Code words in text are shown as follows: "Once we have copied the client files, use `fin.exe` or `finsql.exe` to run the appropriate version of Dynamics NAV."

When we wish to draw your attention to a particular part of a code block, the relevant lines or items will be shown in bold:

```
IF GLEntry.FINDSET THEN
   REPEAT UNTIL GLEntry.NEXT = 0;
```

Any command-line input or output is written as follows:

```
Copy sn.exe -T <assembly>
```

New terms and **important words** are shown in bold. Words that you see on the screen, in menus or dialog boxes for example, appear in our text like this: "There are two options available while installing the Dynamics NAV Classic database server—**Typical** and **Custom**."

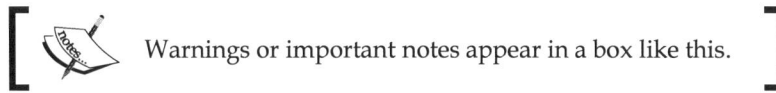

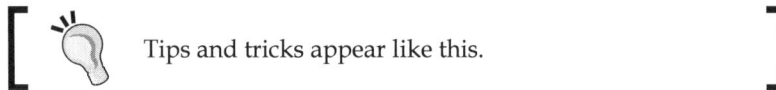

> Warnings or important notes appear in a box like this.

> Tips and tricks appear like this.

Reader feedback

Feedback from our readers is always welcome. Let us know what you think about this book—what you liked or may have disliked. Reader feedback is important for us to develop titles that you really get the most out of.

To send us general feedback, simply send an e-mail to feedback@packtpub.com, and mention the book title via the subject of your message.

If there is a book that you need and would like to see us publish, please send us a note in the **SUGGEST A TITLE** form on www.packtpub.com or e-mail suggest@packtpub.com.

If there is a topic that you have expertise in and you are interested in either writing or contributing to a book, see our author guide on www.packtpub.com/authors.

Customer support

Now that you are the proud owner of a Packt book, we have a number of things to help you to get the most from your purchase.

> **Downloading the example code for this book**
>
> You can download the example code files for all Packt books you have purchased from your account at http://www.PacktPub.com. If you purchased this book elsewhere, you can visit http://www.PacktPub.com/support and register to have the files e-mailed directly to you.

Errata

Although we have taken every care to ensure the accuracy of our content, mistakes do happen. If you find a mistake in one of our books—maybe a mistake in the text or the code—we would be grateful if you would report this to us. By doing so, you can save other readers from frustration and help us improve subsequent versions of this book. If you find any errata, please report them by visiting http://www.packtpub.com/support, selecting your book, clicking on the errata submission form link, and entering the details of your errata. Once your errata are verified, your submission will be accepted and the errata will be uploaded on our website, or added to any list of existing errata, under the Errata section of that title. Any existing errata can be viewed by selecting your title from http://www.packtpub.com/support.

Piracy

Piracy of copyright material on the Internet is an ongoing problem across all media. At Packt, we take the protection of our copyright and licenses very seriously. If you come across any illegal copies of our works, in any form, on the Internet, please provide us with the location address or website name immediately so that we can pursue a remedy.

Please contact us at copyright@packtpub.com with a link to the suspected pirated material.

We appreciate your help in protecting our authors, and our ability to bring you valuable content.

Questions

You can contact us at questions@packtpub.com if you are having a problem with any aspect of the book, and we will do our best to address it.

1
Setting up the Environment for Dynamics NAV

Choosing an **Enterprise Resource Planning (ERP)** solution in today's competitive landscape is not an easy task. A good ERP system is the one, which is rich, robust, and yet flexible to suit current and changing business needs.

Businesses have changed fundamentally in the past decade. Everything from processes to reliance on technology has changed the face of today's businesses. The use of information has become more crucial in fast-changing market trends. The genesis of ERP, CRM, and Business Intelligence systems have made it possible to have business data and information available when, where, and how we need it.

In general the ERP system is referred to as an application or a set of applications and tools that integrate various functions and processes of a company into a single IT system. However, the common perception holds that these systems are fairly expensive and complex. In fact, various studies indicate that more than 50 percent of users already licensed to use these systems never use them. This means a significant amount of a company's investment is wasted on the initial and recurring costs of these systems. The reasons can vary from the choice of a wrong or inherently complex system, highly customized and non-upgradable implementation, to a lack of training, and so on. However, the fundamental piece of an effective business system lies in an imperative synergy between people and processes. These are two significant pieces in every business. While most ERP applications are limited to electronically transforming processes, Microsoft's vision has been to provide a robust business platform by bringing these two worlds together — the world of people and the world of processes.

This can be achieved by combining various aspects. First is a seamless connectivity and integration among various technologies, embedding various pivotal points of personal productivity applications into process systems such as accounting applications or warehouse systems and vice versa. For example, a graphical cost analysis report that tells us about the increasing trend of raw material costs on our mobile device every day, can help us in restrategizing our purchases for the next few months, or creating orders in MS Excel, or simply getting business reports in MS Outlook.

The second aspect is empowering people by giving them the right tools and information they need and making tasks simpler by removing unnecessary and overwhelming information they never use. For example, the information and tools required by a CEO of a company are very different from that of a warehouse worker. However, each business is different and are the roles and responsibilities of people in a business. Therefore, the first and foremost consideration in an ERP deployment is a careful assessment of these roles, functions, and how the ERP system is aligned to them.

In Dynamics NAV, this is achieved by providing a RoleTailored experience to users. The first aspect of seamless connectivity is discussed in the later parts of the book. In this chapter we will focus on the second aspect, which is providing a RoleTailored experience to users and other considerations in deploying NAV.

Considerations for deploying Dynamics NAV

Every organization is different, and so are the deployment requirements of the ERP system. Hence, before deployment of Dynamics NAV, various aspects must be considered, such as the size of the organization, functions of teams and individuals, how they intend to use the system, single or multi-site structure, network requirements, hardware configurations, and so on. We'll start with the first aspect, which is business needs or how the teams and people in our company use the system.

Understanding the business needs of company

Business needs vary for every company and also in every department in a company. As Dynamics NAV is a highly scalable and flexible solution, the deployment requirements can vary extensively between smaller organizations with simple processes versus bigger and more complex operations.

The first and foremost consideration is to decide which areas of our organization will use Dynamics NAV and at what levels. The User Interface design of Dynamics NAV 2009 is centered on the RoleTailored principles. Therefore, before installation and deployment it's important to understand the role of each user or user group, functions they will perform using NAV, and the information they will need. Dynamics NAV comes with various standard user roles. These user roles can be configured, customized, and personalized based on the role group or individual's requirements.

RoleTailored functionality strips away functions that users don't need. This removes unnecessary distractions in their work and brings the information and features they need to the forefront of the system. This helps prioritize tasks and helps users to become more productive in their daily tasks.

Microsoft invested a large amount of resources into finding out what people did in their jobs and how they performed the tasks. The result was that they defined distinct job roles covering essential job functions in areas such as Finance, Sales, Marketing, IT, Manufacturing, and Customer Service. Each job role has a defined list of the functions and features that the individuals need in order to perform their tasks.

Microsoft Dynamics NAV comes with 21 Role Centers out of the box and these are designed to cover the main job roles within a company. However, each user is not restricted to one Role Center and any Role Center can be modified to suit a company's processes.

The following screenshot represents a typical **Role Center** in NAV. It shows the **Role Center** of a "Production planner". Put simply, a Role Center in NAV is a user's personal space in NAV. It shows the most tasks a user usually performs and analysis the user needs, along with the concise information the user needs for his/her role in the company.

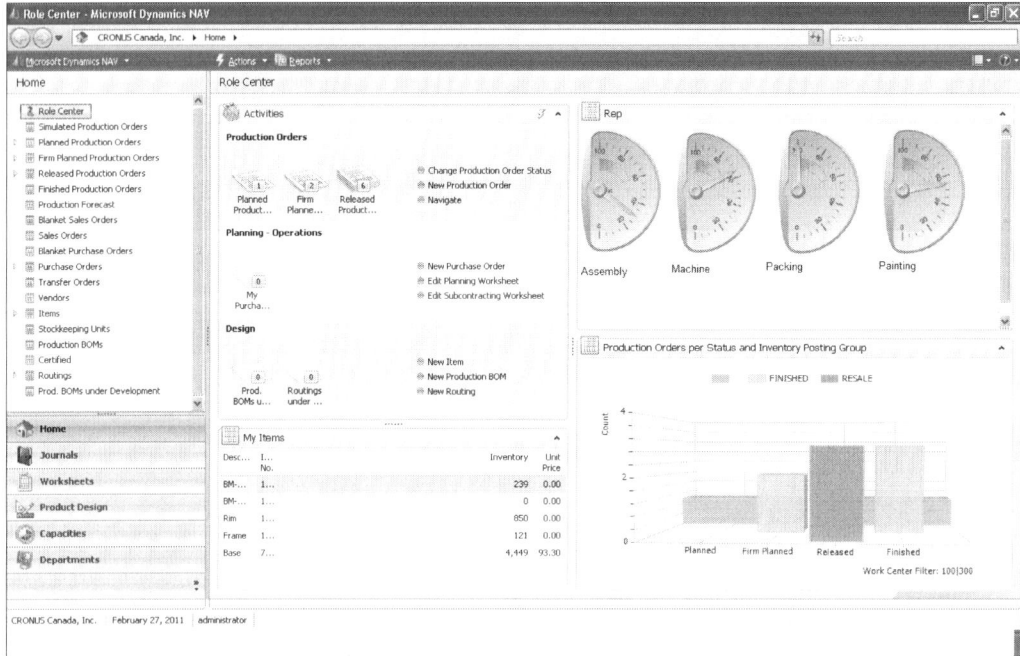

Factors to be considered for configuring a role

The following factors must be considered when configuring a role:

- Pages required for a role, for example, the **Item Card** page or a sales order page

- Structure of the home page and critical or optional information required on the home page

- Procedures and processes required by a role, for example, approval process and more

- Structure of other important pages required for the role

The following screenshots describe how an **Item Card** page differs significantly for two different roles in a company:

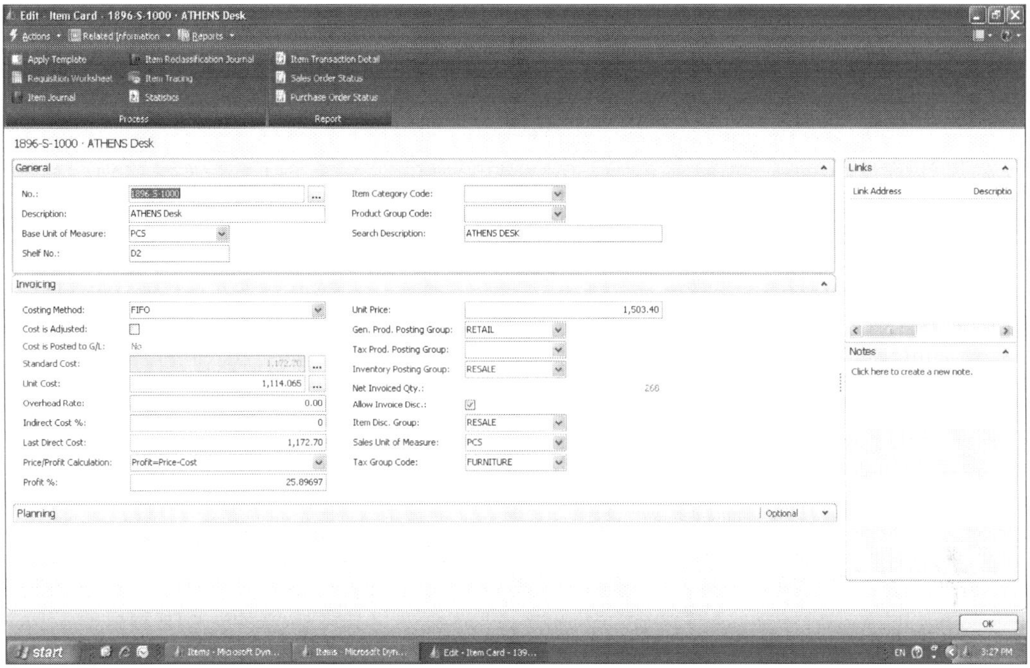
Edit - Item Card - 1896-S-1000 · ATHENS Desk
Actions
Related Information
Reports
Apply Template
Requisition Worksheet
Item Journal
Item Reclassification Journal
Item Tracing
Statistics
Item Transaction Detail
Sales Order Status
Purchase Order Status
Process
Report
1896-S-1000 · ATHENS Desk
General
No.: 1896-S-1000
Description: ATHENS Desk
Base Unit of Measure: PCS
Shelf No.: D2
Item Category Code:
Product Group Code:
Search Description: ATHENS DESK
Invoicing
Costing Method: FIFO
Cost is Adjusted:
Cost is Posted to G/L: No
Standard Cost: 1,172.70
Unit Cost: 1,114.065
Overhead Rate: 0.00
Indirect Cost %: 0
Last Direct Cost: 1,172.70
Price/Profit Calculation: Profit=Price-Cost
Profit %: 25.89697
Unit Price: 1,503.40
Gen. Prod. Posting Group: RETAIL
Tax Prod. Posting Group:
Inventory Posting Group: RESALE
Net Invoiced Qty.: 266
Allow Invoice Disc.:
Item Disc. Group: RESALE
Sales Unit of Measure: PCS
Tax Group Code: FURNITURE
Planning
Optional
Links
Link Address
Descriptio
Notes
Click here to create a new note.
OK
start
Edit - Item Card - 189...
3:27 PM

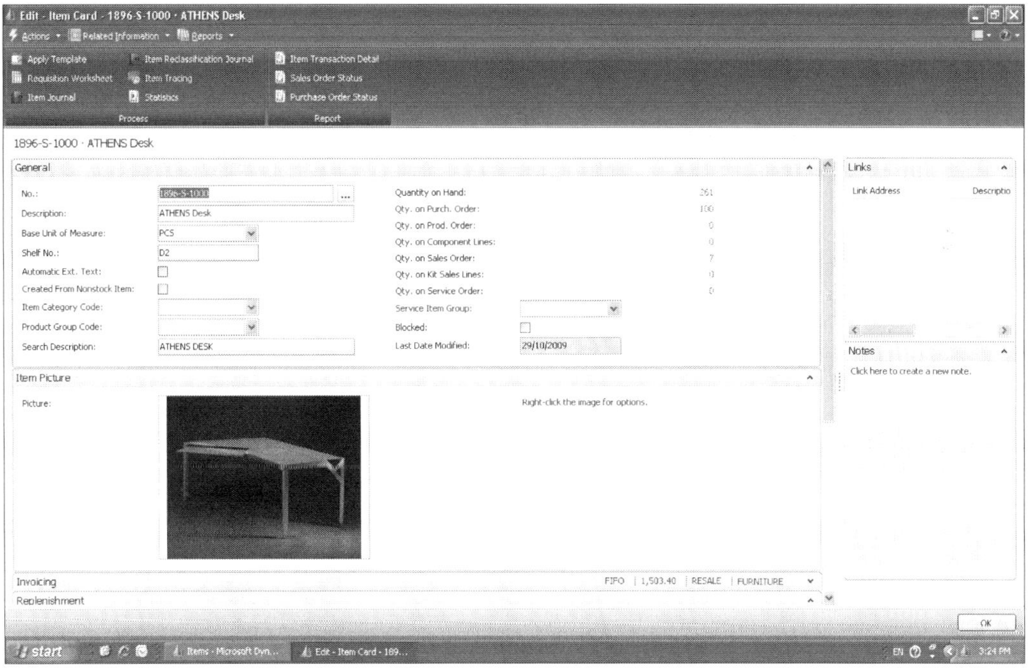
Edit - Item Card - 1896-S-1000 · ATHENS Desk
Actions
Related Information
Reports
Apply Template
Requisition Worksheet
Item Journal
Item Reclassification Journal
Item Tracing
Statistics
Item Transaction Detail
Sales Order Status
Purchase Order Status
Process
Report
1896-S-1000 · ATHENS Desk
General
No.: 1896-S-1000
Description: ATHENS Desk
Base Unit of Measure: PCS
Shelf No.: D2
Automatic Ext. Text:
Created From Nonstock Item:
Item Category Code:
Product Group Code:
Search Description: ATHENS DESK
Quantity on Hand: 261
Qty. on Purch. Order: 100
Qty. on Prod. Order: 0
Qty. on Component Lines: 0
Qty. on Sales Order: 7
Qty. on Kit Sales Lines: 0
Qty. on Service Order: 0
Service Item Group:
Blocked:
Last Date Modified: 29/10/2009
Item Picture
Picture:
Right-click the image for options.
Invoicing
FIFO | 1,503.40 | RESALE | FURNITURE
Replenishment
Links
Link Address
Descriptio
Notes
Click here to create a new note.
OK
start
Items - Microsoft Dyn...
Edit - Item Card - 189...
3:24 PM

Exporting the reporting and Business Intelligence requirements

Business Intelligence (BI) is a mechanism for collecting, analyzing, and providing data using various technologies and systems in order to help business have more visibility and faster access to their data, which will help them make better and faster decisions. As businesses continue to expand across different geographic boundaries, it becomes more important to have visibility and better control.

The Microsoft vision for Business Intelligence is to help drive businesses to improved performance by enabling all decision-makers, essentially empowering all employees throughout the organization to make strong decisions. Microsoft plans to achieve this vision by providing cross-product integration, delivering Business Intelligence capabilities within Microsoft Office, and making its Business Intelligence offerings scalable, therefore everyone in the organization is empowered with Business Intelligence tools. Whether they are working on the strategic, tactical, or operational level, Microsoft Business Intelligence applications can help make informed decisions a natural part of the everyday work experience for all employees.

Microsoft Dynamics NAV is a good example of this cross-product integration and offers a range of Business Intelligence capabilities. It spans from built-in reports and wizards to advanced tools that enable users to gain the insight required to optimize performance across the entire organization. This comprehensive and flexible solution meets the requirements of both small businesses that need easy-to-use yet effective tools, as well as the requirements of larger organizations that need the most technically advanced Business Intelligence capabilities.

> Microsoft Dynamics NAV provides flexible Business Intelligence capabilities and a growth path that enables us to capitalize on our existing investments.

Microsoft Dynamics NAV offers various levels of Business Intelligence depending on our business's needs.

Getting to know the Inherent BI capabilities in NAV

NAV offers strong inherent BI capabilities in the form of an advanced report writer tool; ad hoc filtering, sorting, searching, and charting capabilities throughout the system on any lists; financial reporting tools; MS Excel export, import, and update capabilities, Outlook integration; and personalization of Role Centers.

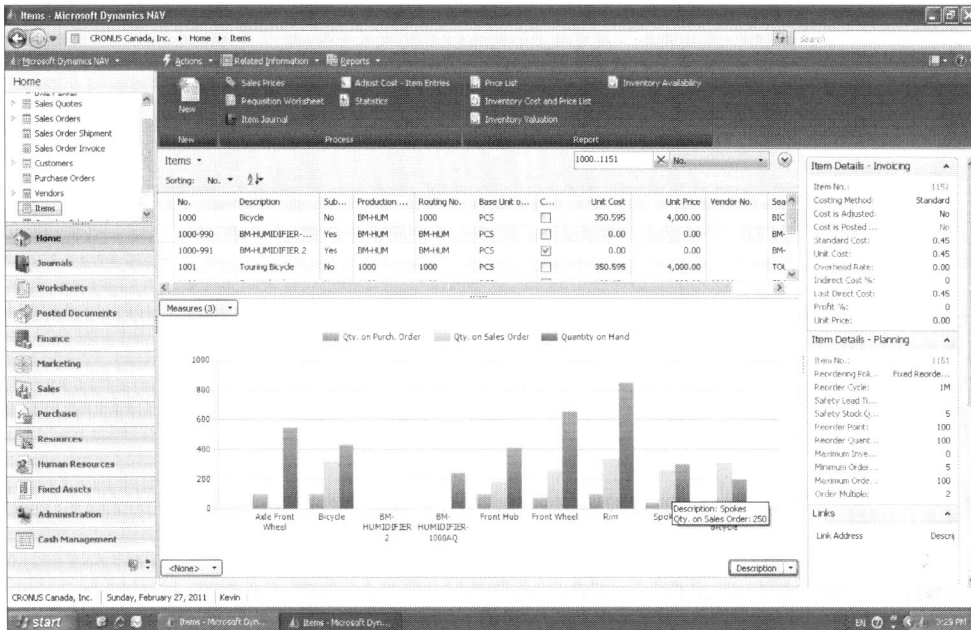

The previous screenshot shows an example of a filtered page with a relevant chart indicating the current status of demand and supply through various parameters such as **Quantity on hand**, **Qty. on Sales Order**, and **Qty. on Purch. Order**.

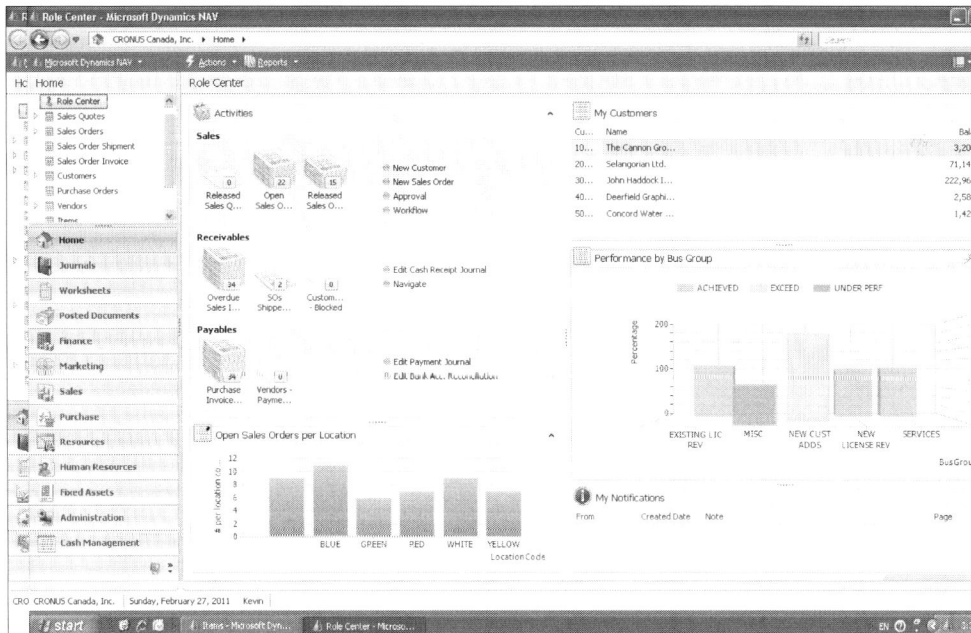

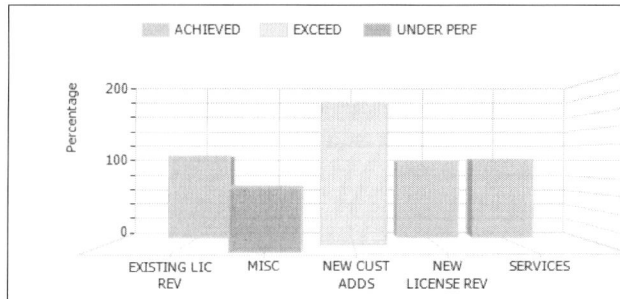

The previous screenshot shows an example of **Role Center** with various charts. Users can add to this to personalize various elements of information they need to see.

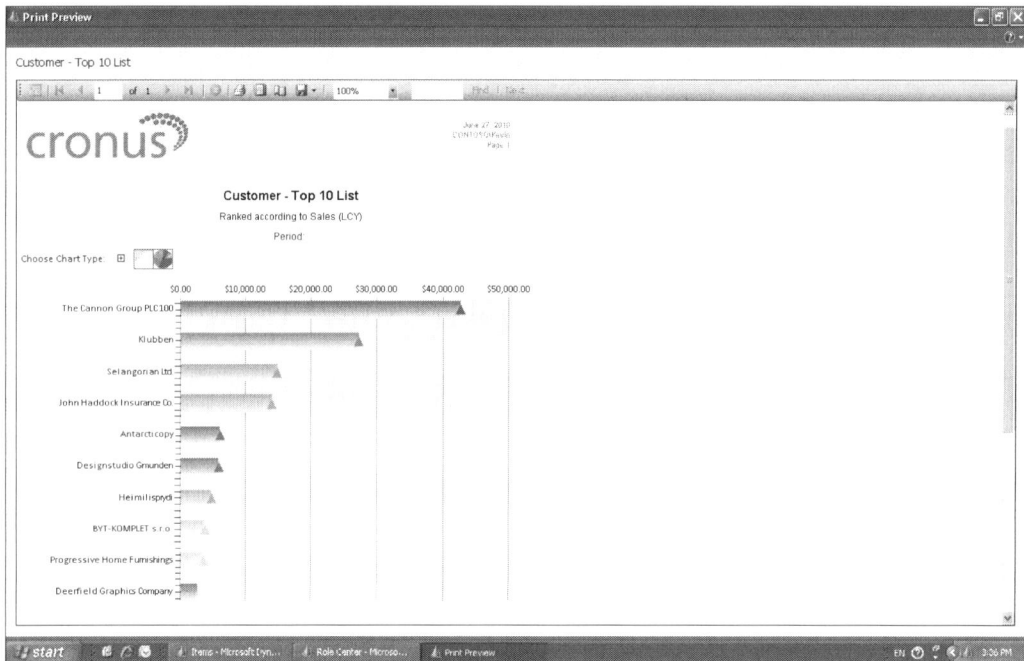

The previous screenshot shows examples of various reports that can be designed using the Dynamics NAV 2009 report writer.

Other BI tools—Business Analytics with NAV

Apart from the inherent BI capabilities in NAV, the users can use **Business Analytics** for more advanced BI requirements. Business Analytics is a dedicated and more advanced form of a Business Intelligence tool built to work seamlessly with Dynamics NAV.

Business Analytics in Microsoft Dynamics NAV delivers information in predefined or easy-to-customize information units called **Online Analytical Processing (OLAP)** cubes, directly to **SQL Sever Analysis Services (SSAS)**.

Users can access and analyze data within a familiar "MS Excel" interface or another frontend solution, which is available with advanced versions of Business Analytics. This solution provides easy-to-use tools that enable straightforward analysis and provide a quick overview of business conditions. Super-users can save and reuse OLAP cubes.

The next screenshot is an example of analysis using the Business Analytics frontend solution:

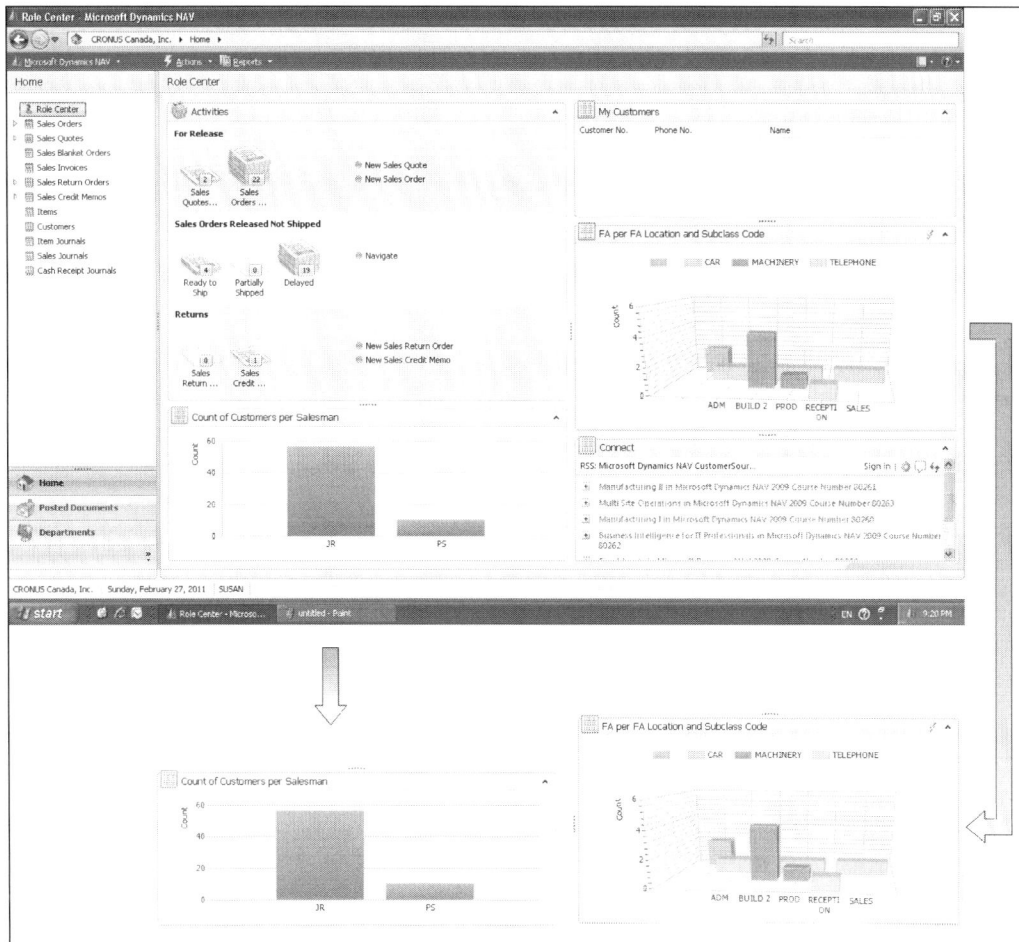

Single or multisite deployment

Dynamics NAV is a very flexible solution to support the varied needs of single or multisite and international organizations. With support for various language packs, multicurrency, intercompany processes, and localizations, it is very easy to deploy NAV across various countries or company locations. However, deployments can be different for every scenario.

Choice of using a single versus multi-database for deployment

In general, a **database** (**DB**) is a simple collection of data. In Dynamics NAV, the data is stored in tables coherently tied to other objects like Forms and Pages. There are six types of objects, namely Forms, Pages, Tables, Codeunits, DataPorts, and XML ports.

The database is then divided into companies. NAV is structured to run various companies in a single database. All companies in a single database follow the structure of the whole DB, which means any design change in any object affects every company in the database. For example, if the developer adds the `SalesTax Discount` field in the sales line table, this field will be available to all companies in that DB.

Now let's see how localizations work with NAV. Dynamics NAV is first released as something called "Worldwide" version or commonly known as W1 version. This is considered the base version of NAV. As it releases across other countries, every region adds a localization layer on top of the W1 version. For example, in the US and Canada, sales tax is used instead of VAT, hence the fields and calculations of taxes will be different from other countries using VAT. This localization layer is added for every region NAV is released in.

> Country/Region country/region-specific documentation can be found through the following link in partnersource:
>
> `https://mbs.microsoft.com/partnersource/documentation/userguides/msdnavlocalfunct.htm`

This implies that multiple countries will require an individual DB of their own, as the objects in a single DB will be the same for all companies in that database. This statement holds true to a large extent but there are some exceptions to the rule.

Let's say our company operates mostly in the US, but has a subsidiary in any other parts of the world where the operations are generally light or are not affected by the local statute changes. For example, this company is used as a warehouse location with simple and low transactions. In this case, the US localization does not affect the operations in this subsidiary nor does the local subsidiary have specific statutory requirements, which can affect the business; thus, using a single DB for this type of scenario might be a preferred choice.

Another example could be that a subsidiary does not have a major local taxation and is used primarily for the export of goods ,which is again not affected by taxes.

Another exception is when the localizations of two databases can be easily merged together in a single database, which should be discussed with our partner and should be carefully assessed. Documents containing details of every region's localizations can be obtained from a certified NAV partner who generally would have the knowledge and experience to recommend the best choice.

Other DB aspects to consider while deploying

The other aspects that we need to consider while deciding between single versus multiple DB are as follows:

- Inter-company operability
- Integration with other systems in headquarters
- License costs

Inter-company operability

Inter-company i**n** NAV is designed for organizations that can have more than one legal business entity and have set up multiple companies to separate functions of each of these entities. The customers and vendors can be set up as business partners in the system and can be assigned intercompany partner codes. It is then possible to exchange complete intercompany purchase and sales documents. The receivables and payables functionality includes the capability of handling multiple currencies, dimensions, automatic conversion of sales orders to purchase orders and vice versa, cross references of item codes, sales and purchase pricing, discounts, and so on.

Integration with other systems in headquarters

Many companies use Dynamics NAV in conjunction with other ERP systems in the company headquarters and Microsoft Dynamics NAV in the various distribution companies abroad. Orders from a distribution company can be transferred from Microsoft Dynamics NAV into the main system. The system receives data, checks its structure, and converts the individual fields into an acceptable format that the parent company can read. It can then be imported as an intercompany order.

Licensing costs

Microsoft Dynamics NAV offers a very flexible and competitive licensing model. The license costs of Microsoft Dynamics NAV depend on four main factors, as follows:

- **Number of users**: Users in NAV are generally referred to as the number of individuals concurrently accessing the system at the same time. Therefore, in an organization of 100 employees only 40 might use the system concurrently, hence only a 40 concurrent users license is required. These are usually full-functional users or heavy users. There are also partial or casual users who are licensed separately as named users (explained in a later section). Therefore, the first step is to determine the maximum number of full functional users that will access the system concurrently.

- **Level of functionality and other requirements**: The second aspect is to determine the functionality we will need for our business. The two basic levels of licensing in Microsoft Dynamics NAV are as follows:

  - **Business Essentials licensing(BE)**: For customers who need core financial management and trade functionality, this edition includes the following:

    - Basic Financial Management (such as General Ledger, A/R, A/P, Fixed Assets)

    - Basic Supply Chain Management (such as sales order processing, purchase order processing, inventory)

    - Basic Business Intelligence and Reporting

    - Basic Configuration and Design tools

  - **Advanced Management licensing(AM)**: For growing, midmarket, or high functional needs. Customers who want a broad set of functionality, this edition includes the following:

    - All functionality included in the Business Essentials Edition

    - Business Intelligence and Reporting

- Manufacturing
- Advanced Supply Chain Management (such as Bill of Materials, requisition management)
- Advanced Financial Management (such as collection, cash management)
- Project Management
- Customer Relationship Management (such as Sales and Marketing in Microsoft Dynamics NAV)

Other requirements: In addition to Business Essentials or Advanced Management, users can buy additional functionality separately, as required by the business. The additional functionality is available in the form of additional modules, which are bought one time, irrespective of the number of users.

- **Nature of usage (Full or partial users)**: In addition to full users, there is also an option of buying partial access for light users. These are users who typically do not use the system heavily but just access only limited parts of the system. Examples could include time entry users, sales people, or executives interested in analysis only. These types of users can be licensed as named users accessing the NAV system through other client options such as MS Excel, SharePoint, or any other external application.

- **Other costs**: Based on our business requirements, there may be additional industry-specific add-ons required with Microsoft Dynamics NAV. For example, an automobile manufacturing company may require a respective add-on built specifically for the automobile industry. These add-ons are usually developed using a Dynamics NAV development environment, thus giving a user a seamless usage experience.

> This section provides a general guidance around licensing costs, but the latest licensing scenarios and costs must be checked with a certified Dynamics reseller.

Integration with external systems and third-party add-ons

NAV provides various integration methods to add-ons and third-party applications. Depending on the requirements, such as real time, online, and offline requirements various methods can be used.

Data ports and XML ports

Data ports and **XML ports** are objects used to export or import data from and to Microsoft Dynamics NAV through external text, XML, or other character delimited files. This type of integration is not real time and requires a manual trigger to initiate the process. This is the simplest form of integration for systems that do not require real-time integration, mostly used with the old versions of NAV when Web services was not introduced. Since the introduction of Web services, integration has become a lot more easier than with earlier methods.

Navision Application Server also known as "NAS"

Navision Application Server was the most common form of integration before Web services was introduced with NAV.

Lot of programmers still use NAS due to its simple design and ease of execution. It is designed to provide access to and from external systems to the NAV database.

Navision Application Server sends and retrieves messages to and from the **Microsoft Message Queue** also known as **MSMQ**. Applications send messages to queues and read messages from queues. It provides efficient routing, security, and priority-based messaging. MSMQ can be used to implement solutions for both asynchronous and synchronous scenarios requiring high performance. Navision Application Server uses API's such as `MSMQBusAdapter.dll` and `NScomcom2.dll` in order to communicate with MSMQ.

Integration using Web services

Web services was introduced with Microsoft Dynamics NAV 2009 and provides the most easy and simplest form of integration to and from other systems. It is a widely known protocol for integration and if someone knows Web services, they can now integrate external systems with NAV without really having in depth knowledge of NAV.

Microsoft Dynamics NAV can expose pages and code units as Web services.

Pages can be exposed as a Web service for external systems to read/write data through **Web Services Definition Language** also known as **WSDL**. A default set of operations can be used by external systems to read, write, modify, and delete data in NAV using default system functions such as read, read multiple, create, create multiple, update, update multiple, and delete. **Codeunit Web services** are exposed as a Web service with no default set of operations, giving the developers the flexibility to decide which operations should be available.

Exploring hardware, operating systems, and networking requirements

This section explains the hardware, operating systems, and networking requirements of the NAV clients, server, and database server. Based on our decision of a centralized or decentralized environment, we will need one or more instances of database installations. We'll start with the requirements for a NAV client.

Dynamics NAV client

Although Dynamics NAV cannot be described as a thin client, in general it is a light application, which can be run on most Desktop PCs, Notebooks, and Net Books. The exact hardware requirements and performance also depend on the OS running on the client machine.

General hardware requirements for default cache settings are as follows:

- 1 GB of RAM (32-bit)/2 GB of RAM (64-bit).
- 1 GHz 32-bit (x86) or 64-bit (x64) Intel or AMD processor.
- Minimum 30 MB of free hard disk space for **RTC** (**RoleTailored client**) and about 110 MB for Classic client. Approximately 140 MB space required for each additional language module to be installed.

The OS requirements are as follows:

- Windows 7 Professional or Ultimate
- Windows Vista Business, Enterprise, or Ultimate with SP1 or SP2
- Microsoft Windows XP Professional SP3

Dynamics NAV server

Microsoft Dynamics NAV server is a .NET-based Windows Service application that works exclusively with SQL Server databases. It uses the Windows Communication Framework as the communication protocol for RoleTailored clients and for Web services. It can execute multiple client requests in parallel and serve other clients by providing Web service access to authenticated clients.

The recommended Operating Systems for Dynamics NAV server are Microsoft Windows Server 2008, Microsoft Small Business Server 2008, Microsoft Windows Essential Business Server 2008 Standard or Premium, Microsoft Windows Server 2003 SP2 or later, Microsoft Windows Server 2003 R2 SP2 or later, and Microsoft Small Business Server 2003 R2 with SP2.

> Microsoft Dynamics NAV runs on both 32-bit and 64-bit operating system editions. It uses **Windows-on-Windows 64-bit** emulation, also known as **WOW64**, on 64 editions, which is a component of the 64-bit Windows OS, capable of running 32-bit applications. Most versions of Windows OS, including Windows Server 2003 and Windows Server 2008, include WOW64 emulation.

Using NAV in WAN configurations

Although there have been various discussions around the use of NAV over WAN connections. the general rule for NAV 2009 is to run the NAV client on Windows RDS (Terminal Services) for WAN connections. The general guideline for the required bandwidth and latency for running the NAV client on RDS over a WAN connection are 24 Kbps per concurrent connection and latency of <= 150 milliseconds.

This, however, might change with the coming versions of NAV where WAN optimization might be included.

WAN options

Windows Terminal Services and Windows Terminal Service with Citrix are the supported solutions for Microsoft Dynamics NAV client running over a WAN connection. Following are the examples of hardware configurations, which can be used for both solutions.

Hardware configurations

10-15 Dynamics NAV users per processor core depending on workload, 64 MB of memory per Dynamics NAV user (assumes an object cache of 32 MB), 1 GB of memory for the Operating System Internal SCSI or SAS RAID, one 10-15K RPM with 500 MB of disk space available for each user, and 1 GB Ethernet connection.

For example, 100 Dynamics NAV users would require as follows:

CPU 100 users / 10 users per processor core = 10 cores or 100 users / 15 users per core = 6.67 cores which really equates to 8 cores.

For this example, a 4-way dual core or 2-way quad core server would be the recommended choice.

Dynamics NAV is utilizing client side cursors; therefore, we may consider smaller Terminal servers for better network bandwidth, such as two 2-way dual core or two 1-way quad core servers.

RAM (100 users X 64 MB per user) + 1 GB for the OS = 7400 MB, which equates to 8 GB of RAM.

For this example if we have deployed a 4-way dual core server all 8 GB of RAM would be installed on that server and the same holds true for the 2-way quad core machines. If we deploy multiple Terminal servers, the RAM calculation is a little different, as we must factor in the 1 GB of RAM for the OS on each server (50 users X 64 MB per user) + 1 GB for the OS = 4200 (4 GB or 6 GB of RAM).

In this example, we will need to take into account workload and activity to decide whether the 4 GB will be sufficient or if we will need to scale up to 6 GB disk. 100 users X 500 MB per user = 50000 MB or 50 GB. For this example, we would recommend two internal 146 GB 15K RPM SCSI or SAS drives in a RAID 1 configuration to hold the Dynamics NAV temp files, OS and program files, page file, and anything else installed on the Terminal server.

It is recommended that we use both calculations.

Networking

The Microsoft Dynamics NAV client requires a 100 MB switched (no hubs) connection to the server. Therefore, 56K modem or broadband connections are not supported with the standard Microsoft Dynamics NAV client. Alternative solutions such as Windows Terminal Services, Microsoft Dynamics NAV Employee Portal, or Terminal Services with Citrix are also available.

Summary

After considering all aspects in a deployment, we are now ready to start installing our ERP software. At this time we are aware of various user requirements such as how NAV will fit our business needs, factors for a decentralized or a centralized environment, Business Intelligence and reporting requirements, and so on. Once we are clear on these aspects, we are now ready to start installing the software for users and administrators. The next chapter explains in depth the various installation procedures and other related criteria.

2
Installing Dynamics NAV

Let's hit the ground running now, and start with the process of actually installing the Dynamics NAV application on the computer. The installation of Dynamics NAV and related components is a little bit more than the standard Microsoft—next, next, next—process. This chapter covers the following:

- Installing the Dynamics NAV Classic client, also called the Dynamics NAV C/SIDE client

- Installing the new Dynamics NAV RoleTailored client (RTC), for NAV 2009 and beyond

- Installing the Dynamics NAV Classic database server also known as the Dynamics NAV C/SIDE database server

- Connecting Dynamics NAV clients to the database server in the lower versions and also the latest NAV 2009 version

The installation of Dynamics NAV Classic components remains more or less similar to the Dynamics NAV 5.0 version. Thus, in this chapter, we have used the NAV 5.0 version for installation of Dynamics NAV Classic components and the Dynamics NAV 2009 SP1 version for installation of RTC and the other new components introduced after the release of NAV 2009.

Installing a Classic client

Classic client installation, also called a **C/SIDE** client, is more or less the same for all the versions of Navision Financials, Navision, Microsoft Business Solutions—Navision, or Dynamics NAV.

We have illustrated an example of 5.0 SP1 Dynamics NAV C/SIDE client installations as follows:

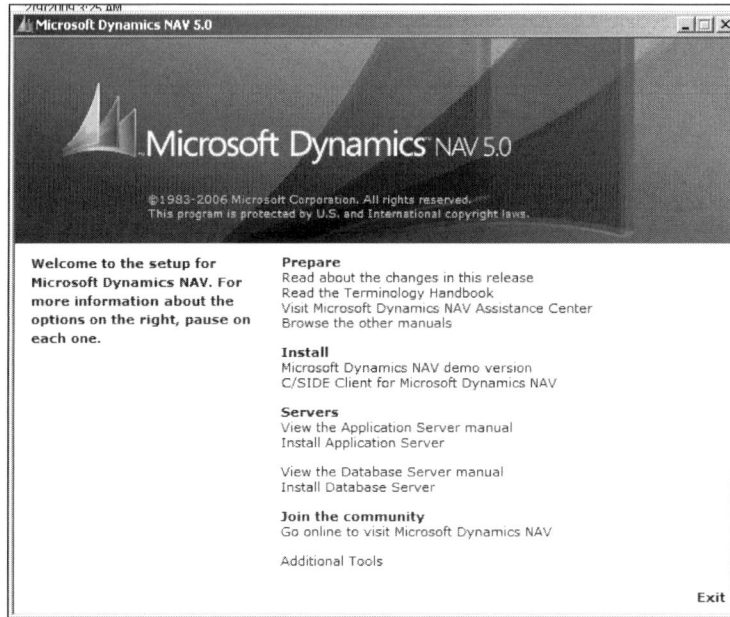

Starting with the startup screen of the installation disk, the process is fairly easy and well defined through the various installation stages. Click on **C/SIDE Client for Microsoft Dynamics NAV** under the **Install** section of the screen to run the installation wizard.

> If we want to install multiple versions of NAV on the same machine, there is a work around to do that. Install the latest version and copy the client (C:\program files\Microsoft Dynamics NAV\...) folder(s) for the rest of the versions that we want to use. Once we have copied the client files, use fin.exe or finsql.exe to run the appropriate version of Dynamics NAV; this is not supported by the standard product and must not be used in a client production environment.

The installation process takes us through the setup wizard. In a network installation, we would typically select **Minimum** as the **Install** option. This needs the least amount of disk space. We can also select this option if we need just the client executables.

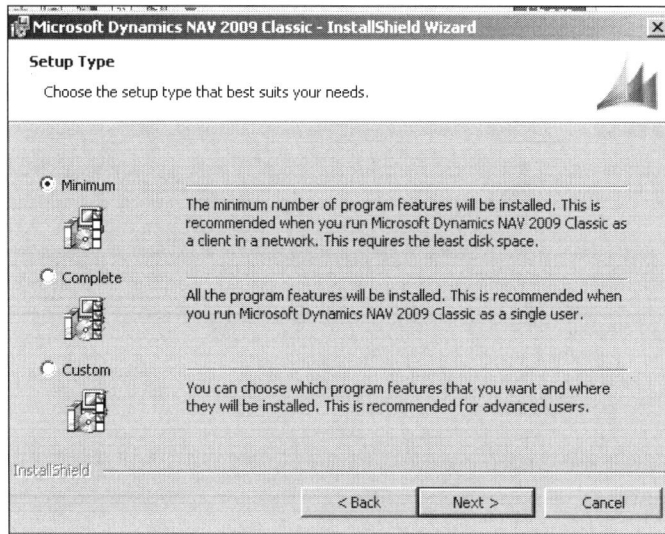

In the following table, the columns indicate the installation options for Dynamics NAV, rows indicate the features available with the option. A checkmark in the respective row and column indicates if the feature is available for that option:

Description	Minimum	Complete	Custom
	Typically used in a network environment. Only with few install options.	All install options selected by default.	Most flexible option and also the one most frequently used. Gives the ability to choose the desired install options.
Help	√	√	√
Demo Database	√	√	√
Backup of Demo Database		√	√
Commerce Integration		√	√
Business Notification Manager		√	√
Employee Portal		√	√
Outlook Integration		√	√
Gantt Server		√	√

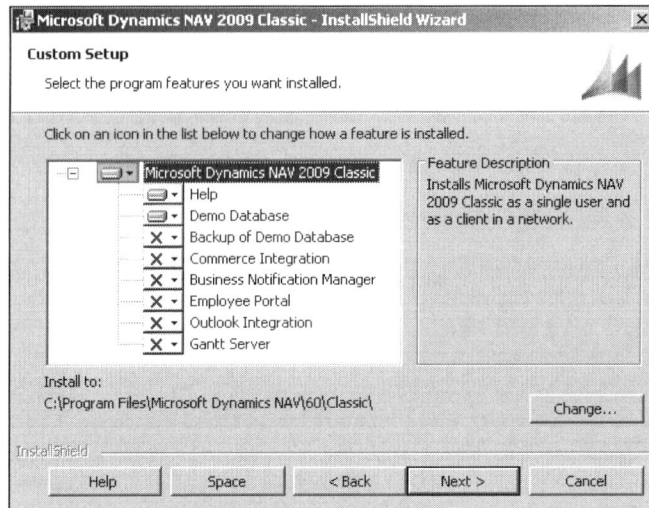

If we select **Custom**, we will get a few options to select from the following:

- **Help**: This is the option for installing Dynamics NAV Online Help. It is recommended to have this option always on.

- **Demo Database**: This is the option to install a demonstration database with the CRONUS company. This is not needed typically in a network installation. We may need to install this option in a single user installation.

- **Backup of Demo Database**: If selected, this option will copy a backup (.fbk file) of the demo database to the program folder.

- **Commerce Integration**, **Employee Portal**: These options need to be selected if we are installing Employee Portal, Commerce Gateway, or Commerce portal (discontinued now) components.

- **Business Notification Manager**: This is the option to send automatic business event notifications from NAV.

- **Outlook Integration**: This feature installs components for Dynamics NAV and Microsoft Outlook Integration. This also installs a toolbar in Microsoft Outlook.

- **Gantt Server**: The OLAP component that facilitates management of shop floor production using visual status updates and plans.

There is also the option to change the installation path, by clicking on the **Change...** button at the bottom.

The following are some of the key program files and what they do:

- `Fin.exe`: This is a client executable for the Microsoft Dynamics NAV C/SIDE client.

- `Finsql.exe`: This is a client executable for the Microsoft Dynamics NAV C/SIDE client for SQL Server option.

- `CRONUS.flf`: This file and the files with extension `.flf` are the license files for Microsoft Dynamics NAV and are responsible for granting appropriate access to the application areas, based on what has been bought from Microsoft.

- `Fin.stx`: The local settings, system menu captions, and regional settings are kept as system text in the `.stx` file.

- `Fin.etx`: The error messages for the system errors and not the application errors generated by business logic are stored in this error text file.

- `Database.fdb`: This is the Microsoft Dynamics Classic database file.

- `Database.fbk`: This is the Microsoft Dynamics Classic database backup.

The wonders of the ZUP file are as follows:

- In the versions prior to Microsoft Dynamics NAV 2009, all local client settings such as column widths, report filters, and displayed form columns, were stored in the `.zup` file for the users on their local application data folder. A parameter for client executables `fin.exe, fin sql.exe — ID=<name>` saves the ZUP file with this ID, thus providing the ability to group the ZUP files together and giving the ability to back up different ZUP files.

- In the Dynamics NAV 2009 RoleTailored client version, the `.zup` file is replaced by the following files and tables where the local settings are stored:

    - `ClientUserSettings.Config`

    - `PersonalizationStore.xml`

    - `CustomSettings.config`

    - Table 2000000075 User Metadata

    - Table 2000000071 Object Mctadata

> **Upwards compatibility**: It is recommended to upgrade the client executables to the latest version, if not the database. However, with NAV 2009 this may not be true.

Installing a C/SIDE database server

A C/SIDE database server has been renamed as the Dynamics NAV Classic database server with the release of Dynamics NAV 2009. This is essentially the Microsoft Dynamics NAV legacy database. The Dynamics NAV Classic database server incorporates the simplicity and easy-to-use features of Microsoft Dynamics NAV. It is a charm to maintain and manage this database. Traditionally, this database server has been used extensively (before the **SQL Express** option was provided). Let's walk through the installation process for this database server, before we discuss some specifics of this server.

We can either select the **Install** option from the auto-run setup for the product CD as shown in the following screen or we can explore the product CD and run `setup.exe` from the `server` folder and follow the installation wizard:

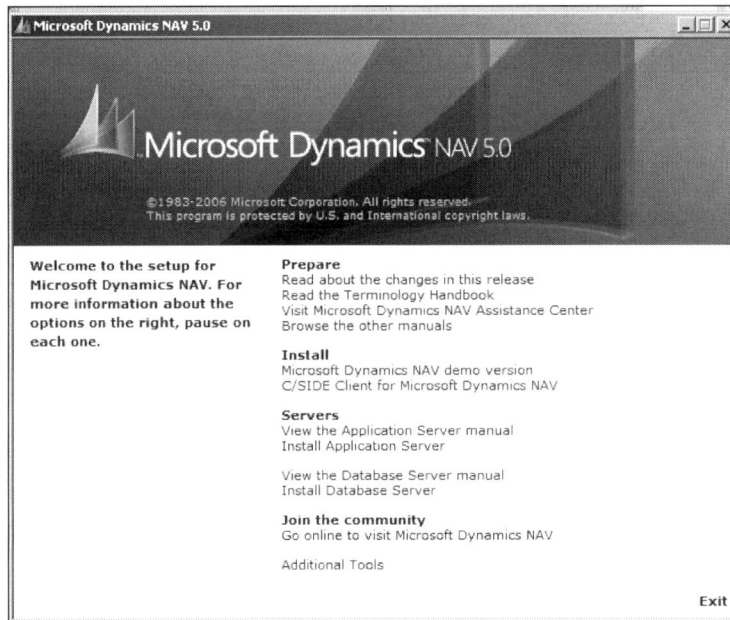

There are two options available while installing the Dynamics NAV Classic database server—**Typical** and **Custom**.

If we select **Custom**, the system will prompt us to enter the following parameters, which are essential for the running of the server:

- **Server Name**: This is the name of the database server. If the name we entered already exists, the installation process will automatically append `#<incremental number>` to the name of the server. For example, if we enter a server name `NAV_DB_Server`, which already exists, the system will automatically rename the server that we are installing to `NAV_DB_Server#1`. This server name is also referenced in the name of the service of NAV database server.

> Spaces are not allowed in the **Server Name** parameter.

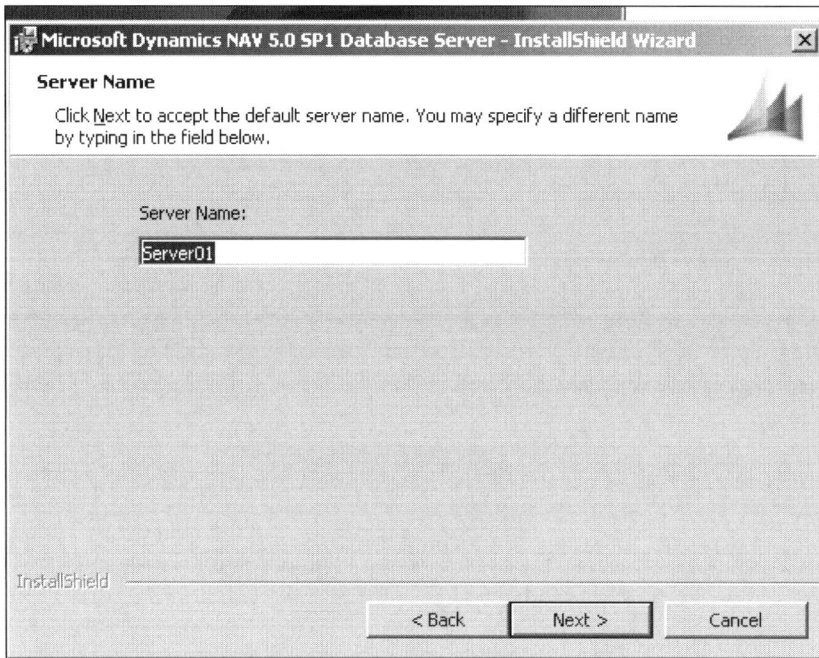

Microsoft Dynamics NAV 5.0 SP1 Database Server - InstallShield Wizard

Server Name

Click Next to accept the default server name. You may specify a different name by typing in the field below.

Server Name:

Server01

InstallShield

< Back   Next >   Cancel

- **Network Protocol**: We will have an option to select from the following network communication protocols:
    - TCP/IP (Kerberos)
    - TCP/IP
    - NetBIOS

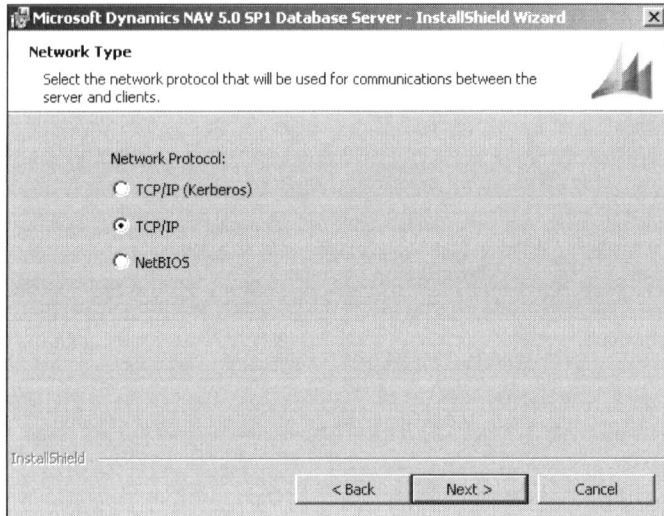

- **Cache Settings**: We will be asked to set aside some space for the cache. There will also be an option to select if commit cache is applicable to the database server.

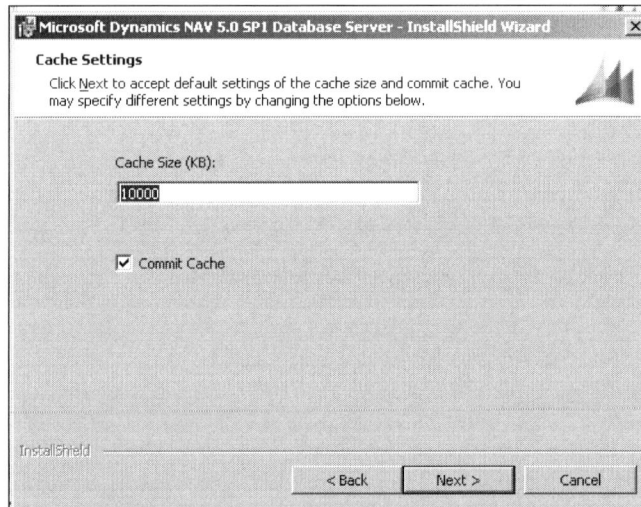

- **License File**: This screen allows us to select the license file. If we select **Install demo license**, the installation will copy the CRONUS.FLF—the demonstration company license file to the server folder and use that for installation. If we select the **Select personal license** option, the installation process prompts us to select a license file path.

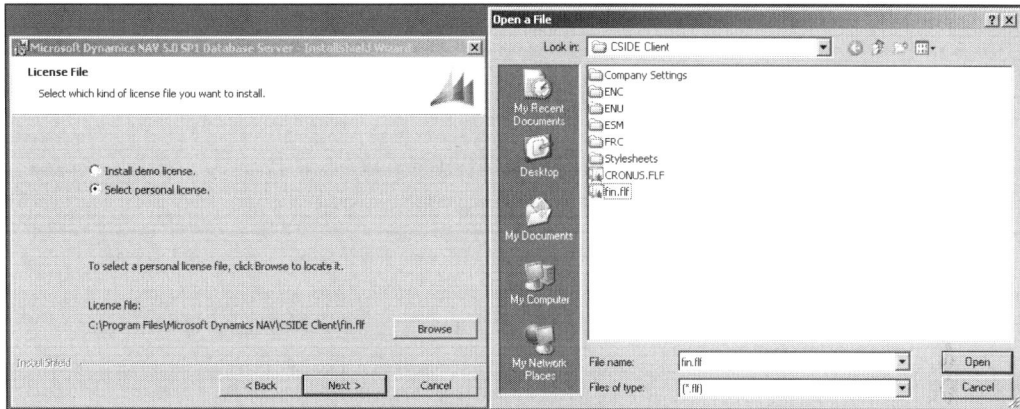

- **Database File**: We get two options here—either to create a database file when the first client connects to the server or select a database file (.fdb) now. If we select the latter, the system would prompt us to select the file path of the database file we intend to use. The next screenshot describes the selection of the database file:

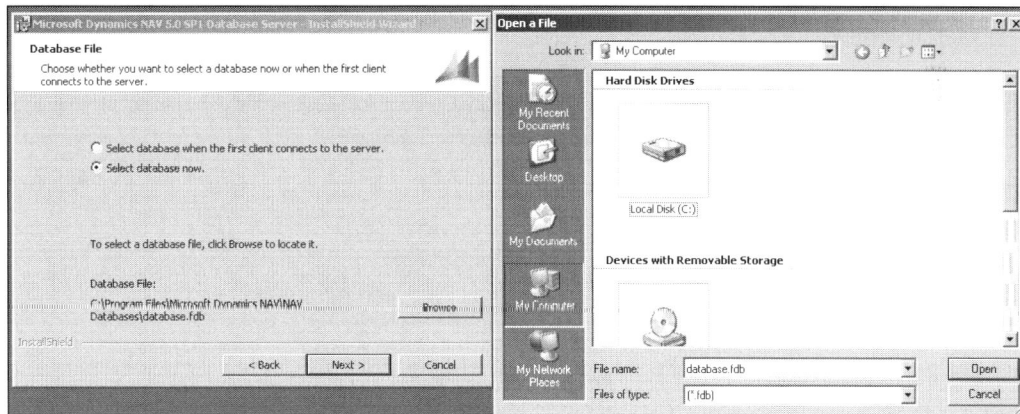

The following table outlines the main parameters as they are selected by default in the **Typical** installation of the Dynamics NAV database server:

	Server Name	**Network Protocol**	**License File**
Typical	Default Computer Name	TCPS	Demo License File
Custom	√	√	√

The following list defines some of the key program files associated with the Dynamics NAV database server and what they do:

- `Server.exe`: This is the executable for the database server.
- `Schemaxt.exe`: This file is used for schema extension.
- `StopSrv.exe`: This is an executable to stop the Dynamics NAV database server service on the computer.
- `HotCopy.exe`: The HotCopy backup utility is a tool that takes a snapshot copy of our database, while the database is still up and running. We can refer to *Chapter 5, Backing up and Restoring Dynamics NAV Database* to know more about this utility.
- `CRONUS.flf`: This is a copy of the demonstration company license.

The Dynamics NAV database server can be used on different configurations and installations. The following command line parameters can be used to set up/change/start/stop the Dynamics NAV database server service and/or installation. These parameters are from Dynamics NAV version 5.0.

Parameter	Client	Server	Description
Server Name	√	√	Used as a client parameter to connect to the server name for the Dynamics NAV database server (as used in the server installation). Used as a server parameter to set the name of the server.
Database	√	√	Used as a client parameter to connect to the database specified in the Dynamics NAV database server installation. Specify the full path of the database file (.fdb) if the database is not stored in the Dynamics NAV folder. Used as a server parameter to set the name of the database.
Company	√		Used as a client parameter to connect directly to a company within the particular server name, database.

Parameter	Client	Server	Description
ID	√		This client parameter is used to define the name for the setup file. The program contains a separate setup/<ID>.zup file every time we connect using a new ID. This parameter is extremely useful in a multiuser configuration, where we can define an ID for every user or a functional group. The program saves Dynamics NAV user settings in a .zup file.
NT Authentication	√		Use this client parameter to specify which authentication will be used to log on to the database/server. The choices are Yes/No. If we select "Yes", the system will use Windows Authentication. Selecting "No" will prompt us to enter a database login and password.
Net Type	√		Use this client parameter to specify the type of network communication protocol that we will be using.
Commit Cache	√	√	Stores writes in the cache before they are written to the database on the server; this makes the database function faster. This can be enabled in both the server and client.
Object Cache	√		This client parameter is used to provide a cache on the client machine for database objects.
Net Type	√	√	Used to specify the type of network protocol that will be used for connecting to the server. It is mandatory to have the same option on both the client and server side. Options are TCPS, TCP/IP, and NetBios
TempPath	√		This client parameter contains the complete path of the temporary file(s) being used by Dynamics NAV while running.
DB Test	√		This parameter is used to test the database when the program is opened. Options are min, max, test.
TestTarget	√		Use this parameter to specify the type of network communication protocol that we will be using.
Status Bar	√		Status bar displays information about the screen (form/table and so on). It also displays whether there is a filter on the screen, the User ID we are logged on as, and work date. This is used as a client parameter.

Parameter	Client	Server	Description
Close Forms on Esc	√		This client parameter determines whether the system closes on pressing the escape key.
Marquee Full Selection	√		This is the option as to where the "whole" control needs to be in the dragged box to be selected or not.
Quick Find	√		This client parameter if enabled by a "Yes", allows us to find the records in an un-editable field as soon as we start writing.
DB Read only	√		Allows the database to be available to the user as read only. This is a client parameter.
DBMS Cache	√		The DBMS cache stores the data in the local system's memory before it is transferred to the database server through the commit cache. The value of the DBMS cache varies from 100 KB to 1 GB. This parameter is used at the client side.
Stoptime		√	Stops the server at a specified time.
Sessions		√	Limits the number of concurrent sessions allowed to log in to the server. The maximum limit is defined by the number of users in the license. This parameter is defined in the server configuration.
Install as Service		√	If we are using the installation wizard to install the NAV database server, the server will be installed as a service by default. This feature comes in handy if we want to install a second instance of the NAV database server on the same physical server.
Uninstall as Service		√	To uninstall the NAV database server service.

Some of the client properties can be changed from **Tools | Options**, as shown in the following window:

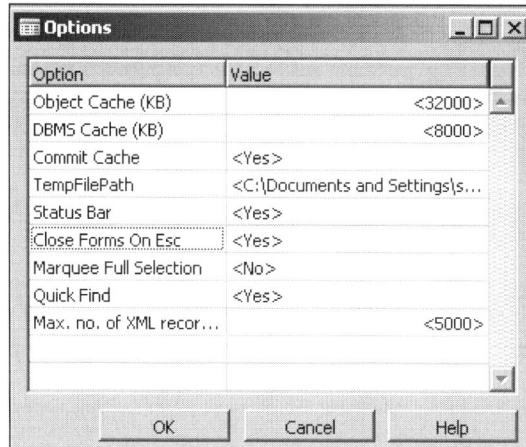

Preparing a Microsoft SQL Server database for Dynamics NAV installation

Though the specifics of setting up a SQL Server database for NAV will be discussed in *Chapter 6, Performance Tuning*, this section describes the raw method of how to do it.

Open the shortcut for the Dynamics NAV Classic client for SQL (`finsql.exe`). Once there, go to **File | Database | New**. Specify the SQL Server name in the **Server Name** field; we may also lookup the SQL Server name with the drop-down **Assist Edit** button provided.

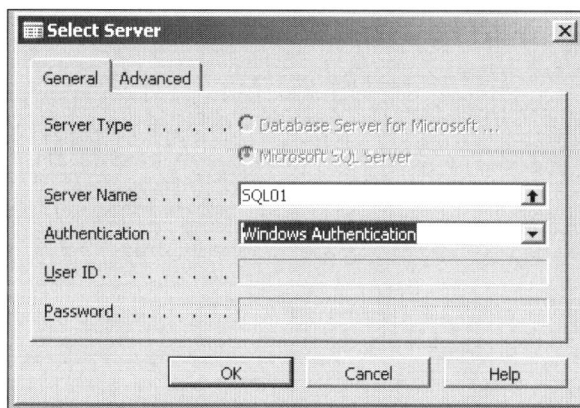

The next option is to select the type of authentication—Windows or Database Server Authentication. If **Database Server Authentication** is selected, the **User ID** and **Password** for the database login will have to be specified. If **Windows Authentication** is selected, the system uses a Windows user login to log on to the SQL Server database. It is worth mentioning that the user selected in this step must have appropriate permissions to create SQL databases.

The next window asks for the database name and shows the following options:

- **The database and transaction log file**: There is an option to select **Location of the files**, **Size**, **File Growth** (amount by which the data file will expand in percentage, MB or KB), **Unexpected Growth** (Yes/No), and **Maximum Size** (MB).
- On the **Collation** tab, the following fields need to be specified:
  - **Windows Collation**
  - **SQL Collation**
  - **Collation Description** (type)
  - **Validate Code Page**

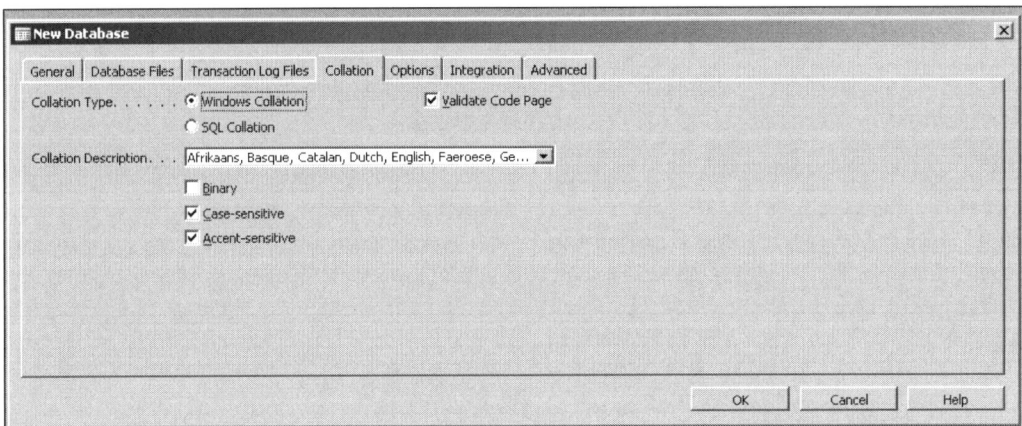

When creating a new database, the SQL Server collation is selected by default (**Windows Collation** *or* **SQL Collation**). It is recommended to select **Windows Collation**, which is closely related to our local, regional, and language settings. We can learn more about Collation in *Chapter 6, Performance Tuning*.

The next tab for **Options** has the following options:

- **Members of db_owner, db_creator, or sysadmin**: This limits access to the database to the users of these three SQL Server roles.

- **Single User**: This setting limits the access of a database to only one login at a time.

- **Recovery Model**: There are three options (**Bulk-Logged**, **Full**, and **Simple**) used for the way that the transaction log is managed for the SQL database:

  ° **Bulk-Logged**: The transaction log will contain information about the large transactions only. This model provides support against disk failure and does not affect the performance as much as the full mode does.

  ° **Full**: The advantage that full log has over all other models is that it guarantees the recovery of the database to the point of failure. It is advisable to use this method for production databases, provided the resources are available to do so.

  ° **Simple**: This is recommended to be used for development databases or non-production databases.

- **Auto shrink**: This provides the option to shrink the database automatically. This operation is performed by SQL Server. This option has had some performance issues associated with it while using with Dynamics NAV.

- **Allow Find As You Type**: This allows us to use find-as-you-type while searching for records in a form.

- **Enable for Microsoft Dynamics NAV Server**: This is a new feature added in the NAV 2009 release; it provides additional support for the new middle tier to be connected to the database.

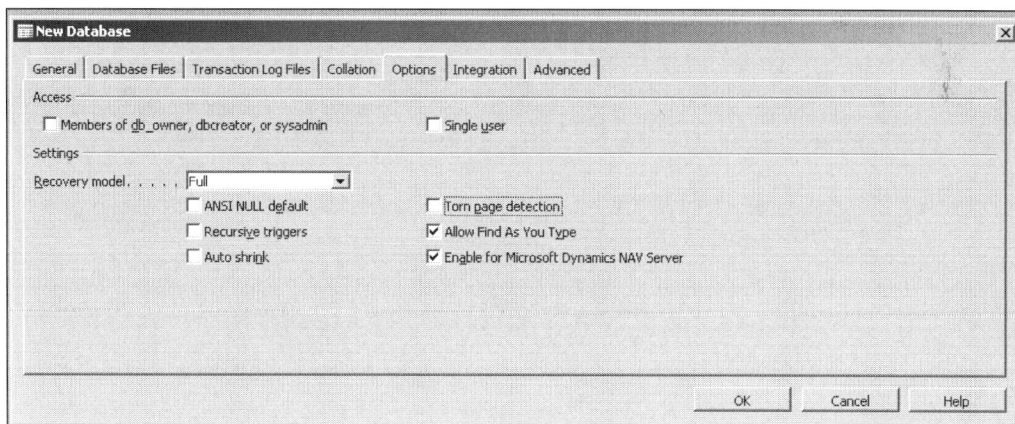

The following set of options is under the **Integration** tab:

- **Maintain relationships**: This determines if the SQL Server will maintain relationships between tables that are defined using the table relations in Dynamics NAV.

- **Save license in the database**: This is an important property that allows the user to save the license in the database. Therefore, if we have multiple licenses that need to be installed on the SQL Server databases, we could store the license in each of the databases instead of storing it in the SQL Server.

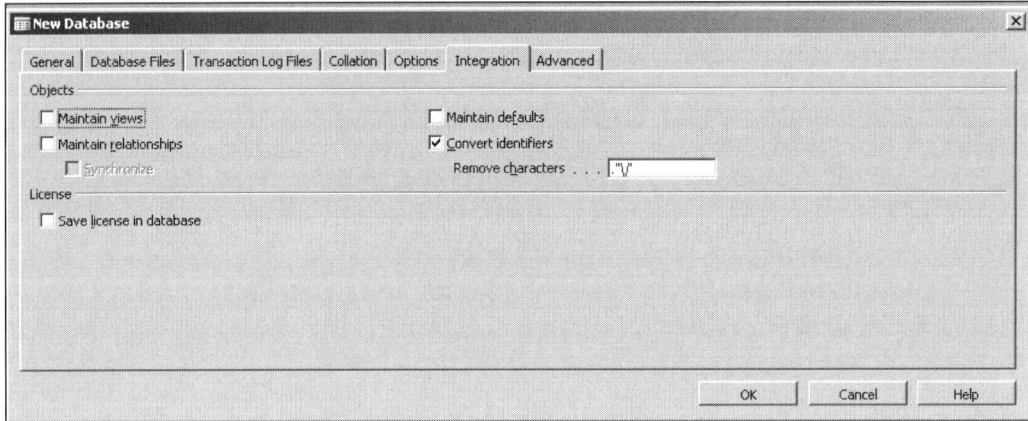

The following set of options is under the **Advanced** tab:

- **Lock timeout**: The user can specify if the client will wait for the locks to be resolved by themselves or it will put a lock on the session that has already been locked.

- **Timeout Duration (sec)**: Specify the time that the session will wait for the lock to clear itself before it locks the session resource.

- **Always rowlock**: SQL will decide what level of locking to choose, if this option is not selected. If this is selected, Microsoft Dynamics NAV will place row-level locks.

- **Security- Models**: Discussed in *Chapter 4*, *Securing Dynamic NAV Applications*.

- **Caching- Record Set**: Define how many recordsets are cached when fetched from the SQL Server using a single FINDSET operation. It will be slower to fetch a recordset that has more than the number specified here, using FINDSET.

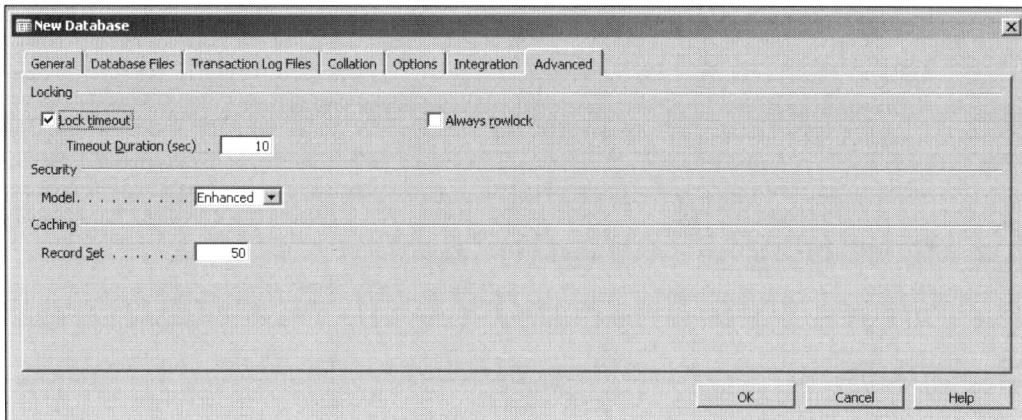

Once all the relevant settings are done and an SQL database created, a backup of the CRONUS database can be restored from the `program files` folder of Dynamics NAV to create a demo database. For more information on how to restore backups, see *Chapter 5, Backups*.

An object file (`.fob`) can also be imported to create a "blank" NAV database.

Connecting a Dynamics NAV client (Classic) to the NAV Classic database server

Open the Dynamics NAV Classic client, also called the C/SIDE client in older versions. Go to **File | Database | Open**.

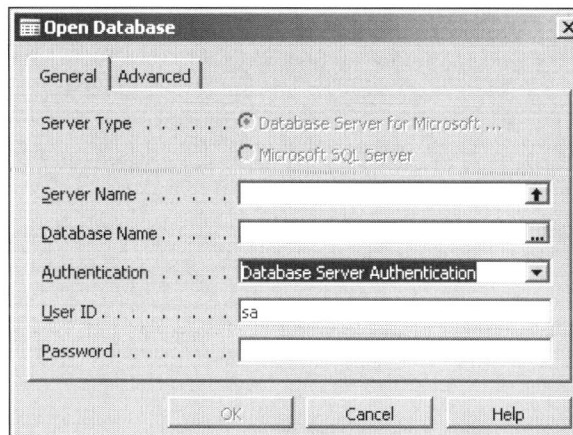

Specify the Dynamics NAV Classic database server name and select the authentication type.

On the **Advanced** tab, there is an option to select the network connection type that we wish to use for the connection to the server.

Connecting a Dynamics NAV client (Classic) to a Microsoft SQL Server database

Click on the Dynamics NAV Classic client for SQL Server (`finsql.exe`) from **File | Database | Open**.

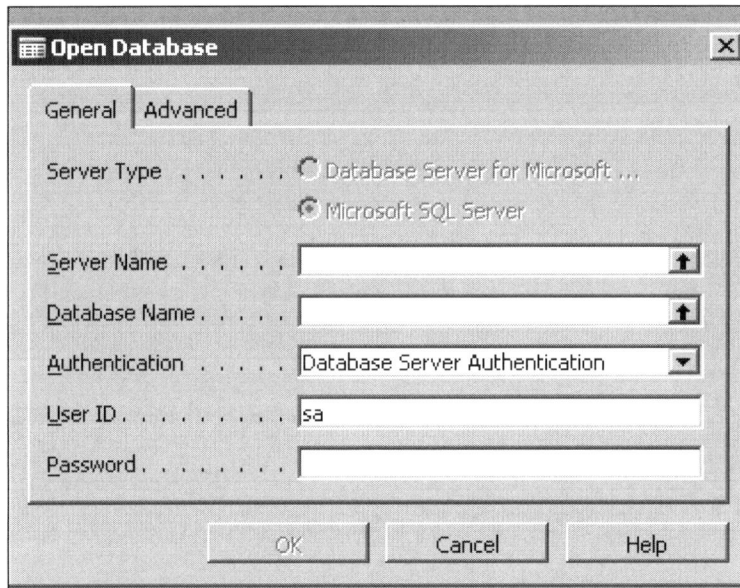

In addition to the SQL **Server Name**, we also need to specify the **Database Name** that we intend to connect to. The next step is to select the authentication type—Windows or Database Server Authentication.

Installing the RoleTailored client for Dynamics NAV

Microsoft introduced a revolutionary client for the Dynamics NAV 2009 and subsequent version called the RoleTailored client for Dynamics NAV. The concept behind this client release is to give an experience to the user of Dynamics NAV, to be able to view their routine tasks and making it a lot easier for them to navigate across the pages and application areas. This is achieved by allowing Microsoft VAR(s), developers, certified consultants, and so on to create Role Centers for the Dynamics NAV users based on their day-to-day tasks. While doing so, an additional layer of application was introduced as a middle-layer component, called Dynamics NAV server. This layer essentially provides an additional level of security for the application and with the use of the Windows communications framework, opens up the application to Web services.

Let's walk through the process to install the Dynamics NAV 2009 RoleTailored client and also the Dynamics NAV server—the middle-tier component.

The setup screen that looks like the following screenshot has different options for different install/configuration types:

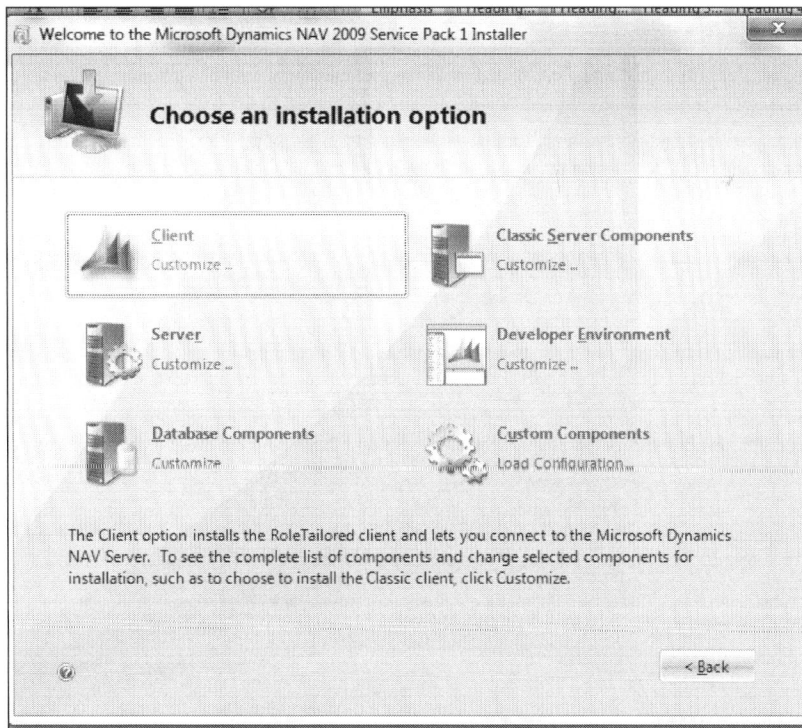

Click on the **Client** if we are installing the NAV client over the network on a user computer. We may have to select the **Developer Environment** or **Classic Server Components**, depending on the type of the planned installation. For more information about types of installations, please refer to *Chapter 1, Setting up the environment for Dynamics NAV*.

If we intend to install additional components, we can choose **Customize** and the following screen will be displayed, which gives us the option to select additional components.

We have to make sure that we have the database server and the NAV server to connect to before installing the NAV RoleTailored client.

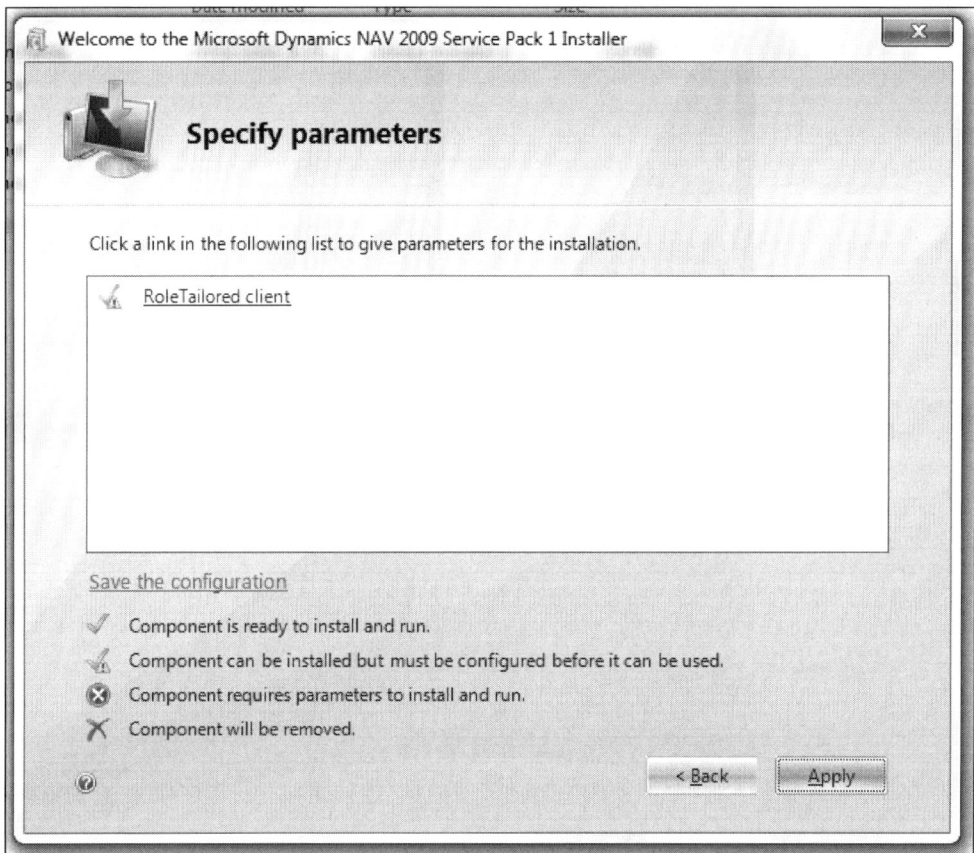

Click on the link and the installation will require us to enter a **Server Name** and communication port.

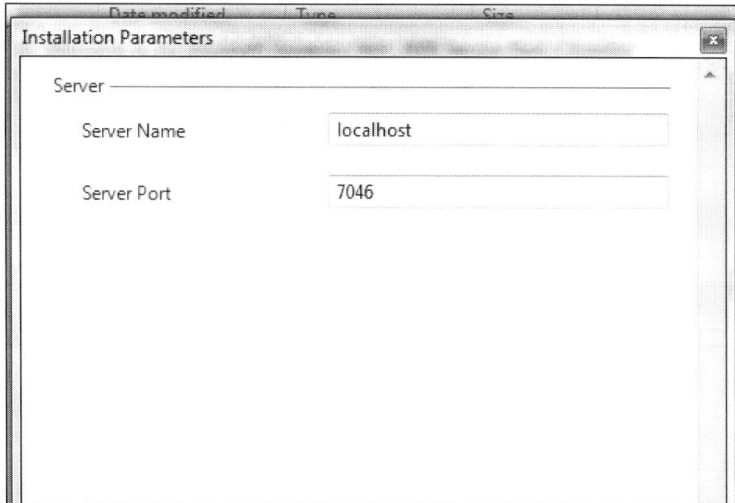

Server Name in the option of the previous screenshot is the Dynamics NAV server name (middle-tier). If we have to change the properties of this connection, we will have to look for the `clientusersettings.config` file and modify the connection details in the file.

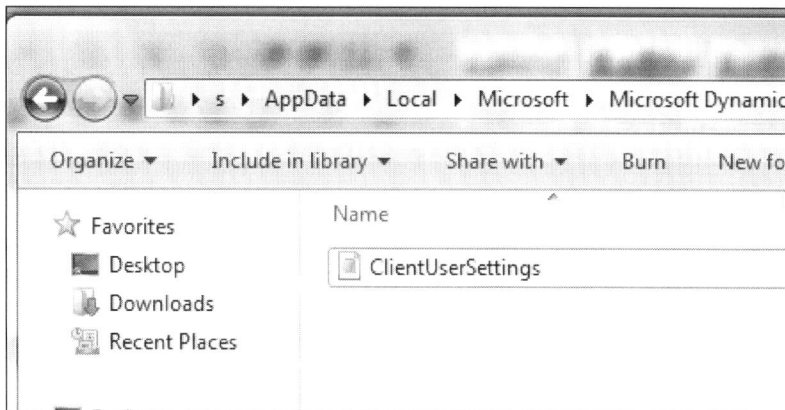

Installing the Dynamics NAV server (the middle-tier component)

Dynamics NAV server is a Windows component service that runs as a middle tier for Dynamics NAV. The middle-tier executes the business logic for the Microsoft Dynamics RoleTailored clients and Web services.

The properties of the connection can be changed at the time of installing the Dynamics NAV server from the installation disk.

After installing the Dynamics NAV server from the installation disk, the properties of the connection are stored in the customsettings.config file as shown in the following screenshot:

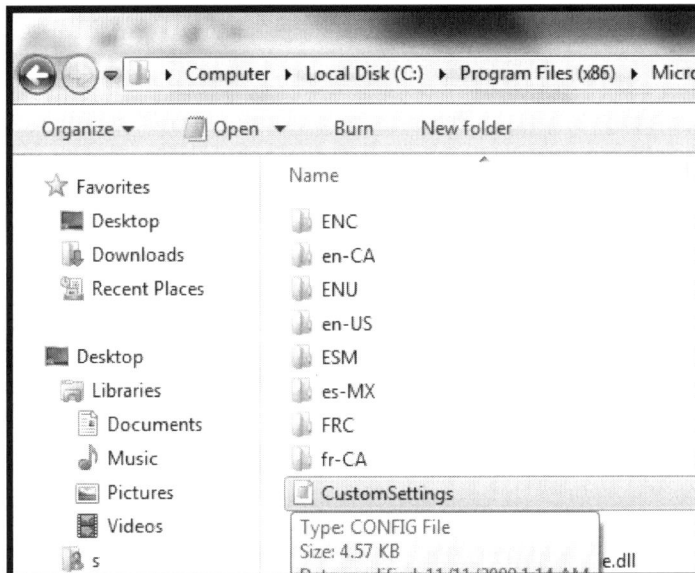

Connecting a RoleTailored client to the database

A Dynamics NAV RoleTailored client connects to the Dynamics NAV server, which in turn connects to the SQL Server database. Essentially, the server name provided at the time of configuring Dynamics NAV connects us to the desired database. We can change the Dynamics NAV server that we are connecting to from the client, by using the option **Select Server**, as shown in the following screenshot:

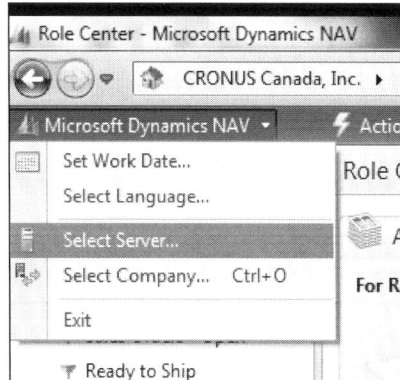

A prompt then asks us for the relevant server address that we intend to connect to and the company in that server's database:

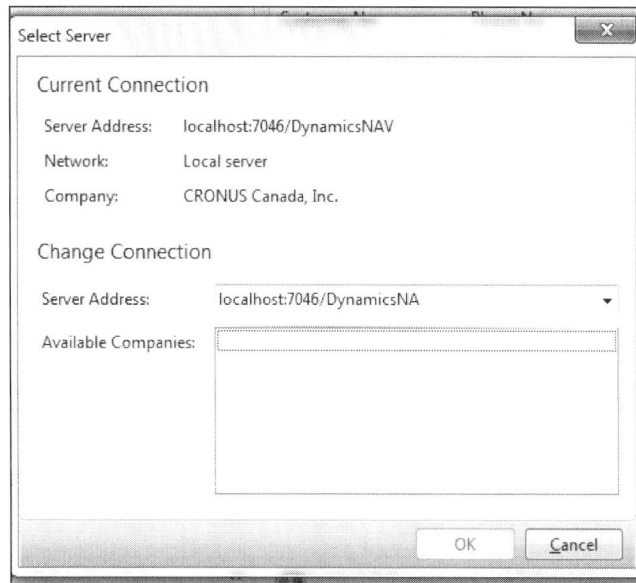

Summary

We saw illustrations of 5.0 SP1 Dynamics NAV C/SIDE client installations. This was followed by an installation of a C/SIDE database server. We then prepared a Microsoft SQL Server database for Dynamics NAV installation. Finally, we connected a Dynamics NAV client to the NAV Classic database server and Microsoft SQL Server database.

We also walked through the process of installing Dynamics NAV 2009 RoleTailored client and also the Dynamics NAV server—the middle-tier component, which gave us additional security to the application. Then we established a connection between the RoleTailored client and the database. We also saw how we can select the appropriate Dynamics NAV server from the client.

3
Integrating Dynamics NAV with the Microsoft Platform

In the previous chapters we have learned the basics of installation and considerations we should take as a user in a Dynamics NAV deployment. In this chapter we will focus on the use of Dynamics NAV with the rest of the Microsoft products and how we can integrate NAV seamlessly to the Microsoft platform. We will talk about various Microsoft technologies, their use, and integration with Microsoft Dynamics NAV.

Integrating Dynamics NAV and the Microsoft Office system

Microsoft Office is perhaps the most successful suite of applications today and undoubtedly the most popular suite of business productivity software. According to researchers, approximately 80 percent of businesses today use some MS Office application in some form. Microsoft Office not only contains various programs but also offers a strong development platform for business applications.

Dynamics NAV with Microsoft Office offers a strong unified business platform with various usage options for users such as the Excel interface and the SharePoint client using **Dynamics Client for Microsoft Office (DCO)**.

MS SharePoint interface

MS SharePoint is a collection of various software elements and services which offer web-based collaboration, workflow management, search capabilities, and a strong document management platform. The SharePoint platform, also known as **Windows SharePoint Services (WSS)**, is a part of Windows Server 2008 and is included with the server license. **Microsoft Office SharePoint Server (MOSS)** offers additional functions and features such as advance enterprise search using a business data catalog, workflow management using InfoPath, advanced content management, and so on.

Dynamics NAV offers strong integration with both WSS and MOSS versions of SharePoint.

Installing and setting up Microsoft Dynamics NAV Employee Portal

Employee Portal acts as a bridge between Microsoft Dynamics NAV and SharePoint, making it easy for our employees to work with critical business information. With Employee Portal, our employees use a web-based interface for the following:

- Getting quick updates of real-time business information, such as invoices, customer data, and reports
- Modifying information, which is immediately updated directly in our business system

Employee Portal is intuitive and requires a minimum of programming. It comes with four out of the box Microsoft .NET-based Web Parts, and it is easy to configure on the Microsoft Dynamics NAV backend. The four standard Web Parts available with Employee Portal are as follows:

- Card Type
- List type
- Header Type
- Lines Type

The following diagram shows the architecture of Employee Portal with NAV:

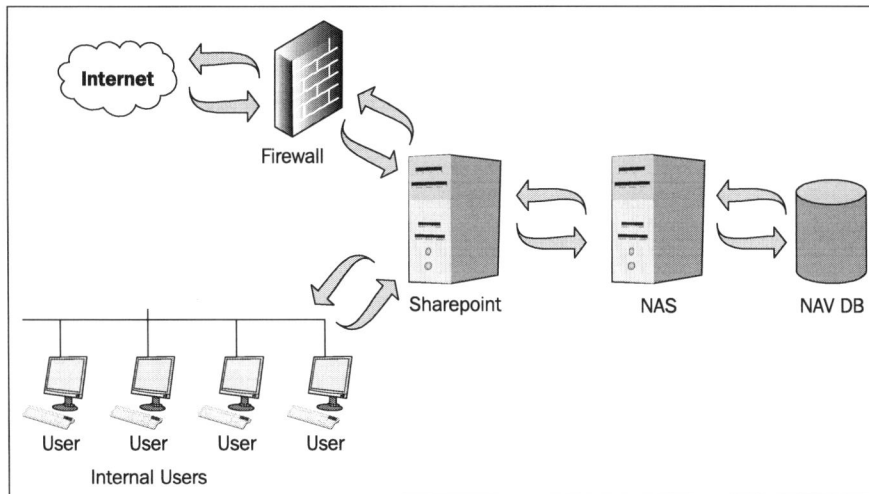

Installing Employee Portal

Employee Portal can be configured to display NAV data through any browser with SharePoint. The following steps show installation and configuration of Employee Portal with NAV:

1. Before installing the **Employee Portal** frontend components, make sure that the following backend components are installed. If not, we need to follow the instructions in the previous chapter for installation of these components.

    °   Dynamics NAV database server or SQL option

    °   Dynamics NAV C/SIDE client (at least one instance of Classic client option for configurations and setups)

    °   NAV Application Server

2. In the NAV client installation, we must make sure that **Employee Portal** is included in the options of installed components.

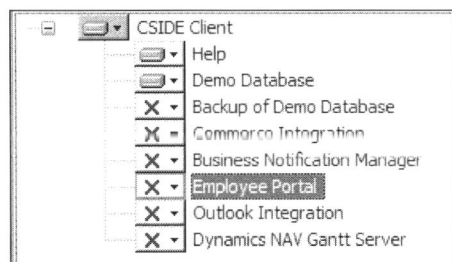

3. The previous screenshot lists all the available options in a NAV client installation. Select **Employee Portal** to be installed if our setup looks like the previous screenshot.

4. Similar to the NAV client installation, the Navision Application Server must have the **Employee Portal Components** installed as well.

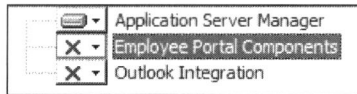

5. The previous screenshot shows NAS installation without **Employee Portal Components**, which is the default setup.

6. Choose custom installation and select **Employee Portal Components** to be installed. Employee Portal uses NAS for all communication and NAS is based on the Microsoft Message Queue protocol.

7. All request queues and reply queues should be installed on the computer hosting NAS and on the server hosting SharePoint respectively.

8. Set up a user profile for this instance of Employee Portal. Name the user, for example, **NEP_user (Navision employee portal user)**.

9. The following screenshot shows the NAS configuration for the **NEP_user**:

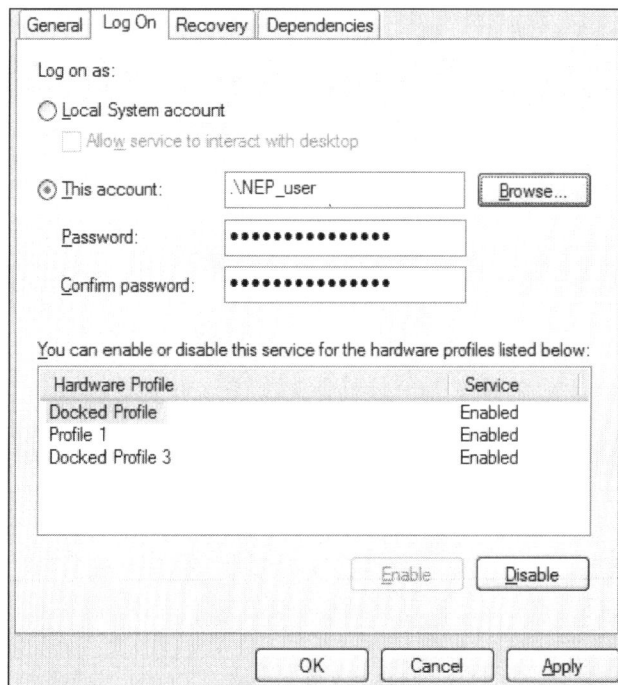

Installing other required software

The other software that need to be installed are as follows:

- Microsoft .NET Framework
- Microsoft Message Queue Services
- Microsoft Visual J# .NET Framework Redistributable Package

While Microsoft .Net Framework and Microsoft Message Queue Services are available as a part of Windows Server 2003 and Server 2008, Microsoft Visual J# .NET Framework Redistributable Package can be downloaded from the following link at the Microsoft download center. We need to check the download center for the latest links to available downloads:

```
http://www.microsoft.com/downloads/details.aspx?familyid=f72c74b3-
ed0e-4af8-ae63-2f0e42501be1&displaylang=en.
```

Installing Employee Portal frontend components

Locate the employee portal installation program in the product CD for NAV 2009. The installation wizard guides us through the installation and requires us to enter the basic information such as company name, user name, and so on. In the **Server Name** window, as shown in the following screenshot, we can enter the name of the computer that hosts the backend message queue, which Employee Portal communicates with:

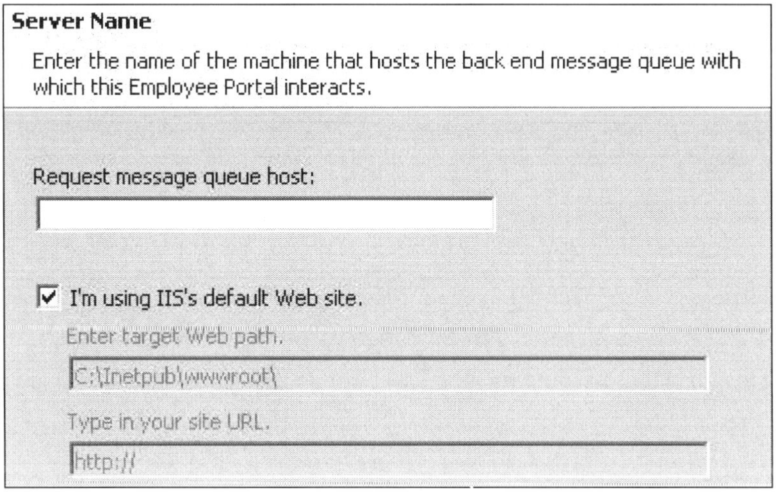

We must make sure that the following components in the screenshot, including **Demo Site**, are installed. If we choose **Complete** in the installation type, all these components will be automatically installed.

As a result of the installation, a new virtual directory has been created and a Web Part pack containing the Web Parts developed for **Employee Portal** have been copied together with other required resources.

Next is how to set up **Employee Portal** and create a **Demo Site**. The first step in setting up **Employee Portal** is to configure NAS for **Employee Portal**. NAS for Employee Portal using message queue is the engine for communicating between NAV and SharePoint. An application server record in Dynamics NAV should be created for the **Employee Portal** instance of NAS. Other application server records must be created for each application server instance setup.

The General tab

The next screenshot shows the **General** tab information of the application server setup. In the **General** tab we have the following settings:

- **Code**: This field accepts alphanumerics up to 10 characters, and must start with **NEP-1** for Employee Portal
- **Description**: Enter the description using up to 30 characters
- **Use Encryption**: Used to activate encryption of the data sent from Dynamics NAV to the frontend
- **Use Compression**: Used to activate compression of the data sent from Dynamics NAV to the frontend

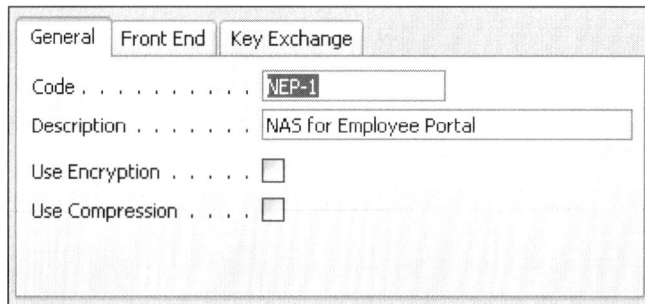

The Front End tab

The **Front End** tab has the following settings:

- **Front End Processing**: A check mark in this field will enable this application server to handle the communication between Dynamics NAV and the frontend.

- **Request Queue**: Enter the path of the message queue handling the messages coming into Dynamics NAV, for example, `.\private$\nep_request_queue`.

- **Reply Queue**: Enter the path of the message queue handling the messages going out of Dynamics NAV, for example, `.\private$\nep_reply_queue`.

The Key Exchange tab

The following screenshot shows an example of all fields filled in the **Key Exchange** tab:

- **Handle Key Exchange**: A check mark in this field will enable the application server handle the trust requests from the frontend.

- **Key Exchange Request Queue**: Path of the message queue handling the messages coming into Dynamics NAV from trusted sites, for example `.\private$\request_encryption`.

- **Key Exchange Reply Queue**: Path of the message queue handling the messages going out of Dynamics NAV to trusted sites, for example, `.\private$\reply_encryption`.

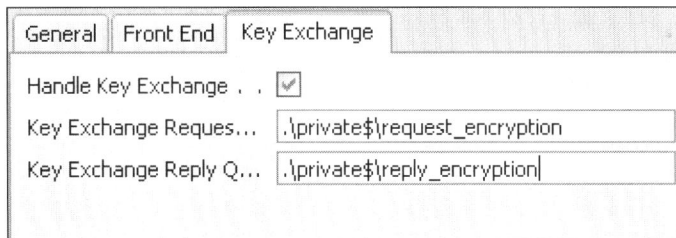

General	Front End	Key Exchange

Handle Key Exchange . . ☑
Key Exchange Reques... `.\private$\request_encryption`
Key Exchange Reply Q... `.\private$\reply_encryption`

Setting up captions

Captions must be defined in the Employee Portal setup for the test to appear on the Web Parts. At least one caption must be defined for each of the following elements: Group Captions, Web Part Request Captions, Web Part Table Tab Captions, Web Part Table Action Captions, and Web Setup Captions. Let's take an example of creating Web Part Table Tab Captions. The procedure for creating other captions is exactly the same.

1. Open the caption list of the **EP WP Table Tab Caption List**.
2. Click **Caption | Create New**.
3. Select the language for the caption.
4. Enter the caption in the **Caption** field.

The language code can be the same for all lines or different, depending on how many languages are being used. A translation for each language with a different language code must be defined for each language used for the same caption.

Creating Web Part Request templates

A template in **Employee Portal** is an instance of a Web Part Request containing the basic definitions of a Web Part Request. It can be used as a model for creating many Web Part Requests. It contains formatting of tables and tabs and, sometimes, lookups and sort keys. However, actions for interaction and navigation must still be filled in on the individual Web Part Request.

Web Part templates are also used to define actions. If this is the case, the Web Part type is **System**.

We must select the type of the Web Part Request to define how the data is presented in the Web Part.

The types are as follows:

- **List**: To show a list of records
- **Card**: To show a record in a card
- **Header + Line**: To show a header with attached lines
- **System (for actions)**: These Web Part Requests are predefined by the program and can only be used for actions

Setting up users and groups

A collection of Web Part Requests is called a **group** and users must be assigned to a group. Once assigned, all settings of the group are inherited over except the language ID. The language ID should be defined if multiple languages are used and each user language preference is different.

In the group window, press *F3* to create a new group. Fill the following fields in the group card header and lines:

- **Code** and **Description**: Enter the code and description for the group, for example, **PRODUCTDESIGN** and **Product Design Group** respectively.

- **No. of WP Requests**: Contains the number of Web Part Requests connected to the group. The field is updated automatically from the number of lines entered in the previous section.

- **Caption**: The caption that will show in the tool pane when we configure the Web Part on our portal page.

General					
Code	PRODUCTDESIGN				
Description	Product Designers Group				
No. of WP Requests. . .	9				
Language ID	4105				
Language Name.	English (Canada)				
Caption.	Product Design				

	Code	Description	Editable	T...	Defined b...	Caption
	ITEMCARD	Item Card	✔	C..		Item Card
	ITEMLIST	Item List		L...		Item List
	PRODBO...	Production BOM Card		H..		Productio..
	PRODBO...	Production BOM List		L...		Productio..
	PRODBO...	Production BOM Version Card	✔	H..		Productio..
▶	PRODBO...	Production BOM Version List		L...		Productio..
	ROUTIN...	Routing List		L...		Routing Lis
	UOMLIST	Unit of Measure List		L...		Unit of M...
	VENDOR...	Vendor List		L...		Vendor List

Once these elements are set up, we can now view our page by opening a web browser and browse to the **Employee Portal Demo Site** at `http://localhost/default.aspx`.

Exporting documents to MS Excel and MS Word

With release of version 5.0 in NAV, Microsoft introduced an excellent feature of exporting all documents to either MS Word or MS Excel with a click of a button. Of course, copying and pasting was always available, but never before was exporting the documents so easy. By simply clicking a button, Microsoft Dynamics NAV can generate an XML document that exports the available information to either MS Word or MS Excel. This is done using stylesheet templates, which are already built for NAV 2009 Classic forms and NAV 2009 RoleTailored client (RTC) pages. If we want to modify these templates or stylesheets, it can be done using a stylesheet toolkit and can be done with a little knowledge of XML and C/AL programming.

Imagine we are working with an open list in NAV and we want to export this list to MS Excel. By simply clicking a button, the entire page with all filters, range, and columns intact will be exported to a formatted Excel sheet with a worksheet for each **Header** tab and a worksheet for lines.

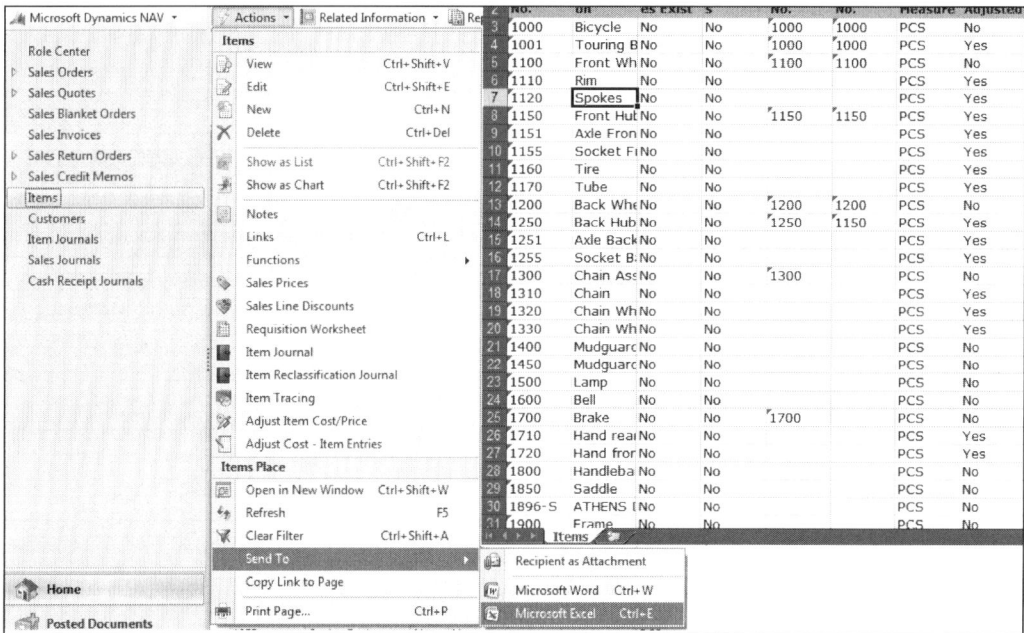

The **Send To** Word or Excel function can be found under the **Actions** menu on any page in NAV. Clicking this link will export the page in a formatted Excel worksheet, as shown in the previous screenshot.

Creating a Customer Card stylesheet for MS Word

NAV offers flexibility to customize or create new stylesheets according to our personalized formats. This can be done using a stylesheet toolkit available through our customer source access. We can download the toolkit from the following link. We must check the customer source for latest updates on links and versions to download at the following link: `https://mbs.microsoft.com/customersource/ downloads/servicepacks/NAVStyleSheetTool`.

Once the toolkit is downloaded, unzip it and find the `Style Sheet Tool 2.0.fob` file for the NAV objects. Open the NAV Classic client to import all objects in our DB. Use the **Replace ALL** option to replace all the conflicting objects or to create new objects.

In this example, we will create a new **Customer Card** stylesheet.

To create a new stylesheet for the **Customer Card** and make the information on the item card available in Word, let's complete the following steps:

1. From the **Object Designer**, point to **Forms** and run **Style Sheet Card** (form 680).

2. Click **Insert** on the top menu or press *F3* to create a new blank record.

3. Fill the **Code** and **description** fields with the relevant stylesheet code and a description of the stylesheet, for example **Customer Card**. The **code** and **description** fields can contain a maximum of 10 and 50 characters respectively.

4. In the **Form No.** and the **Page No.** fields, select the form and page we want to use and the table associated with it, for example use **21** for the customer form and customer page.

   (A form is used in the Classic client and an associated page is used in the RoleTailored client.)

5. In the lines select the relevant **Table No.**, for example we can use **Customer** or **table18**. Select **Base Record** as **Yes** in this line, as this will be the base data item for the styelsheet. Select **Fields** from the next stylesheet menu and choose the fields we want to use in this stylesheet. Once the fields are selected, the **Fields Selected** box will be automatically checked.

The following screenshots show how the field selection lines and the stylesheet form respectively should look after the selections have been made:

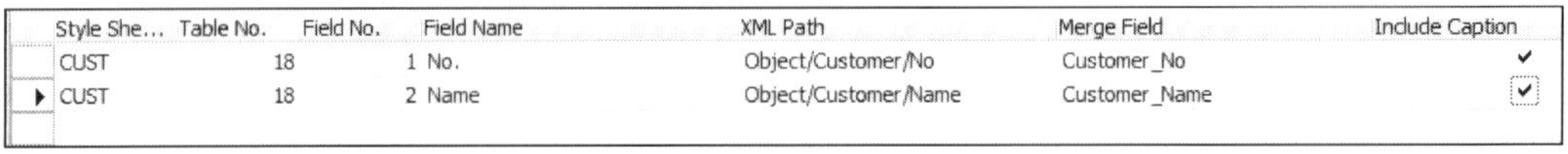

Style She...	Table No.	Field No.	Field Name	XML Path	Merge Field	Include Caption
CUST	18	1 No.		Object/Customer/No	Customer_No	✔
CUST	18	2 Name		Object/Customer/Name	Customer_Name	✔

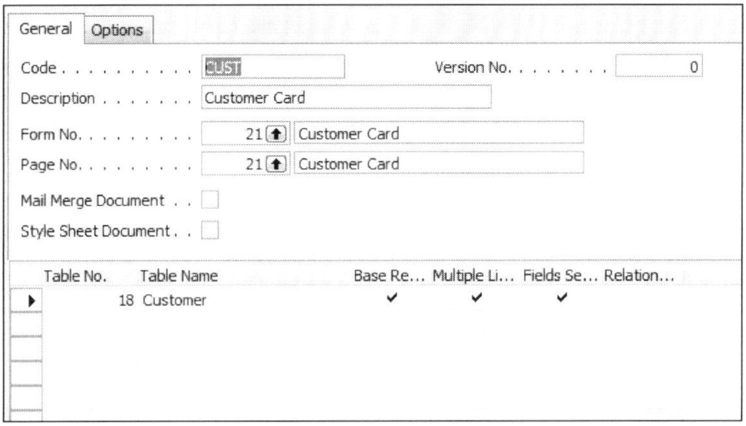

General | Options

Code	CUST		Version No.	0
Description	Customer Card			
Form No.	21 ⬆	Customer Card		
Page No.	21 ⬆	Customer Card		
Mail Merge Document . .	☐			
Style Sheet Document . .	☐			

Table No.	Table Name	Base Re...	Multiple Li...	Fields Se...	Relation...
▶ 18	Customer	✔	✔	✔	

The fields to use for this **Customer Card** and page have now been defined and we are ready to merge the selected fields into a Word document as **Mail Merge** fields.

Creating a Mail Merge with the Customer Card stylesheet

1. As per the previous screenshot, on the stylesheet card that we just created, click **Create Mail Merge** from the following stylesheet menu:

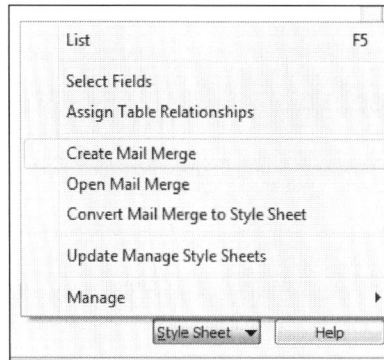

2. In Word, click **Mailings | Insert Merge Field** and select each field one at a time.

3. Design the document as necessary by adding our own text and pictures. The following screenshot shows an example of what the Mail Merge could look like:

4. Close Word when we are finished and return to Microsoft Dynamics NAV.

5. Click **Yes** to import the Mail Merge document and to convert the Mail Merge document to a stylesheet document.

6. Click **Yes** to update **Manage Style Sheets**. This will associate the stylesheet we just created with the **Customer Card** and Customer page.

7. In Microsoft Dynamics NAV, on the main menu, click **Sales & Marketing, Order Processing & Customers** to open the **Customer Card**.

8. Click the **Send to Word** button to export the **Customer Card** to the newly created Word document format.

Using extensibility with NAV 2009 SP1

With Microsoft Dynamics NAV 2009 SP1, we can now use the RoleTailored client control add-ins to extend the RoleTailored client with custom functionality built using Visual Studio. A control add-in is a custom control, including visual elements, for displaying and modifying data on RoleTailored client pages. The following screenshot shows use of an external component in the RoleTailored client:

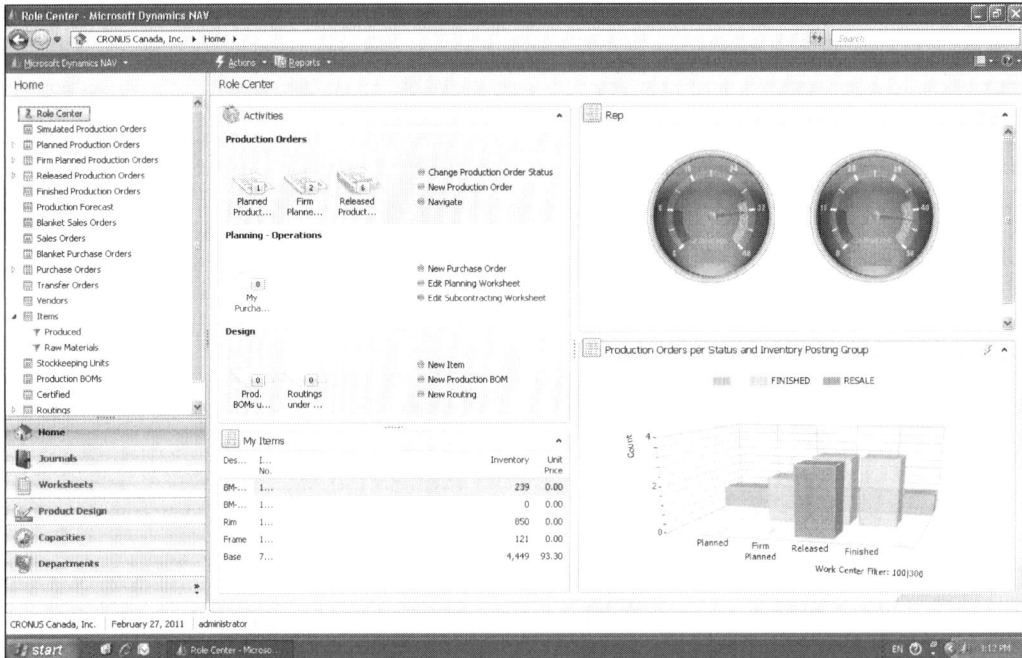

Using a control add-in on pages

We can use control add-ins on field controls of RoleTailored client pages and they can be used on more than one field control on a page.

We can use control add-ins on pages that are included in parts and FactBoxes of other pages.

We can design the user interface of the control add-in to fill the page part area entirely or partially.

Control add-ins cannot be used on the following areas:

- Action pane
- Command bar
- Filter pane

Example of using an add-in on RTC

In the following example, we will see how to use a **SQL Reporting Service** (**SRS**) report part in a RoleTailored client.

The first step is to create an SRS report using a standard NAV dataset. Use Visual Studio to design this report using the NAV database. After the report is designed, build and deploy the report.

In order to use the report in RTC, we need to use Internet Explorer as a container to run the report. The following code runs an IE page in the RTC. Notice the path of the IE page is the path of the required report with toolbar visibility as `false`.

```
ieInstance.Navigate("http://localhost/ReportServer/Pages/ReportViewer.
aspx?%2
fBI+Reps-
AM%2fTop+Custs&rs:Command=Renderhttp://localhost/
ReportServer?%2fBI+Reps-
AM%2fTop+Custs&rs:Command=Render:Toolbar=false");
base.OnVisibleChanged(visible);
```

Microsoft Dynamics NAV 2009 includes the `Microsoft.Dynamics.Framework.UI.Extensibility.dll` assembly that defines the model for creating RoleTailored client add-ins. The API provides the binding mechanism between the RoleTailored client add-in and the Microsoft Dynamics NAV 2009 framework.

Creating add-ins

To create the add-in, let's perform the following steps:

1. In Visual Studio Express, Visual Studio 2005, or Visual Studio 2008, create a Visual C# project type using the Class Library template.
2. Name the solution `NAV_IE`.

3. In the project, add references to the following assemblies:

   ○ `Microsoft.Dynamics.Framework.UI.Extensibility.dll` assembly: By default, the path to the assembly is `C:\Program Files\Microsoft Dynamics NAV\60\RoleTailored client`. This reference is required for all RoleTailored client add-ins.

   ○ `System.Windows.Forms`: This contains classes for creating user interfaces for Windows-based applications.

   ○ `System.Drawing`: This provides access to basic graphics functionality.

4. Open the `Class1.cs` file and add the following `using` directives:

```
using System;
using System.ComponentModel;
using System.Collections.Generic;
using System.Linq;
using System.Text;
using System.Drawing;
using System.Windows.Forms;
using Microsoft.Dynamics.Framework.UI.Extensibility;
using Microsoft.Dynamics.Framework.UI.Extensibility.WinForms;
```

5. Add the remaining following code to our C# program. The complete code should look like the following:

```
using System;
using System.ComponentModel;
using System.Collections.Generic;
using System.Linq;
using System.Text;
using System.Drawing;
using System.Windows.Forms;
using Microsoft.Dynamics.Framework.UI.Extensibility;
using Microsoft.Dynamics.Framework.UI.Extensibility.WinForms;

namespace NAV_IE
{
  [ControlAddInExport("NAV_AddIn_Explorer")]
  [Description("An embeded IE instance")]
  public class NAVExplorer : WinFormsControlAddInBase
  {
    WebBrowser ieInstance;
```

```
    protected override System.Windows.Forms.Control
CreateControl()
    {
      ieInstance = new WebBrowser();
      //MessageBox.Show("Create Control");
      return ieInstance;
    }
    protected override void OnVisibleChanged(bool visible)
    {
        //MessageBox.Show("visible changed");
        ieInstance.Navigate("http://localhost/ReportServer/Pages/
ReportViewer.aspx?%2fBI+Reps-AM%2fTop+Custs&rs:Command=Renderht
tp://localhost/ReportServer?%2fBI+Reps-AM%2fTop+Custs&rs:Command=R
ender:Toolbar=false");
        base.OnVisibleChanged(visible);
    }
    protected override void OnInitialize()
    {
      //MessageBox.Show("On Initialize");

      base.OnInitialize();
    }
    public override bool AllowCaptionControl
    {
      get
      {
        return false;
      }
    }
  }
}
```

6. Notice the commented `MessageBox` lines. We can remove the comments to debug and test the code.

7. Sign the add-in assembly. An assembly must be signed to be used in the RoleTailored client. Open the project's properties.

8. On the **Properties** window, click **Signing,** and then select the **Sign the assembly** checkbox.

9. In the **Choose a strong name key file** box, select <**New**...>.

10. In the **Key file name** box, type NAV-TE.

11. Build the solution.

Registering the add-in in Microsoft Dynamics NAV

To register an add-in, we include it in the client add-in table in Microsoft Dynamics NAV. To include an add-in in the table, we must provide the following information:

- **Add-in name**: The add-in name is determined by the `Microsoft.Dynamics.Framework.UI.Extensibility.ControlAddInExportAttribute` attribute value of the add-in class definition that we specified when creating the control add-in. The name in this example is `NAV-IE`, as shown in the code.

- **Public key token**: This is a 16-character key that is given to the assembly when it is signed and built in Visual Studio. To determine the public token key, run the Microsoft .NET **Strong Name Utility** (**sn.exe**) on the assembly. The `sn.exe` utility is available with the Visual Studio 2005 and Visual Studio 2008 SDKs.

- **To determine the add-in's public key token**: At a command prompt, change to the directory that contains the `sn.exe` utility. For example, the default directory for Microsoft Visual Studio 2008 is `C:\Program Files\Microsoft Visual Studio 8\SDK\v2.0\Bin`.

Type the following command:

```
Copy sn.exe -T <assembly>
```

Replace `<assembly>` with the add-in assembly's path and file name, such as `Program Files\Microsoft Dynamics NAV\60\RoleTailored Client\Add-ins\NAV-IE.dll`.

We need to enter and note the public token key that is displayed:

1. Once the add-in is registered, it's now required to add the control in the table and then on the RTC page.

2. Open the **object designer** and create a new table with at least one picture field of type BLOB.

   For example, create a table with ID: 50001 and name it `Test-IE`. Create two fields—Pic with types code and BLOB.

3. Now create a blank page, for example with ID 50019, call it `Rep-1`. Create the sections as shown in the following screenshot:

Name	Caption	Type	SubType	SourceExpr
General	<General>	Container	ContentArea	
Pic	Views	Field		Picture
		Container	ContentArea	

4. Keeping the cursor on the empty line, click **View | Properties**. The **Properties** should include the newly created source table, as shown in the following screenshot:

Property	Value
ID	
Name	Rep-1
Caption	Rep
CaptionML	ENU=Rep;ENC=Rep
Editable	<Yes>
Description	<>
Permissions	<Undefined>
PageType	CardPart
InstructionalTextML	<Undefined>
CardFormID	<Undefined>
DataCaptionExpr	<Undefined>
RefreshOnActivate	Yes
PromotedActionCategoriesML	<Undefined>
SourceTable	Test-IE
SourceTableView	<Undefined>
InsertAllowed	<Yes>
ModifyAllowed	<Yes>
DeleteAllowed	<Yes>
DelayedInsert	<No>
MultipleNewLines	<No>
SaveValues	<No>
AutoSplitKey	<No>
DataCaptionFields	<Undefined>
SourceTableTemporary	<No>
LinksAllowed	<Yes>
PopulateAllFields	<Undefined>

5. Close this view and go back to the sections. Now placing the cursor on the **Pic** section, view the properties. This should display the properties of the **Pic** section. Lookup the **ControlAddIn** property and choose the registered add-in. Once the add-in is selected, it should look like the following screenshot:

Property	Value
HideValue	<FALSE>
Caption	Views
CaptionML	ENU=Views;ENC=Views
MultiLine	<No>
ToolTip	<>
ToolTipML	<Undefined>
Description	<>
OptionCaption	<Undefined>
OptionCaptionML	<Undefined>
DecimalPlaces	<Undefined>
Title	<No>
MinValue	<>
MaxValue	<>
NotBlank	<No>
CharAllowed	<Undefined>
ValuesAllowed	<>
BlankNumbers	<DontBlank>
BlankZero	<No>
AutoFormatType	
AutoFormatExpr	<>
SourceExpr	Picture
TableRelation	<Undefined>
Importance	<Standard>
CaptionClass	<>
DrillDownFormID	<Undefined>
LookupFormID	<Undefined>
Lookup	<Undefined>
DrillDown	<Undefined>
AssistEdit	<Undefined>
ClosingDates	<No>
Numeric	<No>
DateFormula	<No>
ControlAddIn	NAV_AddIn_Explorer;PublicKeyToken=aa7dd275b4fc3b56
Style	<None>
StyleExpr	<FALSE>

6. As the part is created with the add-in, it can now be added to any RTC page by designing the page and adding a section with this newly created part.

7. Now we are ready to use any SRS report within our RTC page.

Summary

In this chapter we have seen how Dynamics NAV is integrated with the rest of the Microsoft Stack, including SharePoint and other Office applications. Another advantage of using NAV with SharePoint is that light users (users who don't use the system for large transactional type activities) can just use the Web interface with SharePoint, using the Dynamics Client for MS Office (DCO) license and not the full concurrent license, more details of which are explained in the licensing chapter of the book.

4
Securing Dynamics NAV Applications

In this chapter, we will discuss the NAV Security Architecture including security recommendations and best practices. Securing our applications is of paramount importance these days. Security becomes even more critical when it is our organization's financial data that needs to be protected.

Essentially, there are a few components of securing the Dynamics NAV application. They are as follows:

- Network security
- Hardware security
- SQL database and Classic database security
- Dynamics NAV access — roles, users, logins, and permissions

Securing the network is essential to any organization's IT security. Firewalls and implementing user security policies go a long way in securing the network. A few highlights of network/hardware security that we will not cover in detail in this chapter are as follows:

- Implementing Dynamics NAV on a secure internal company network.
- Following Microsoft recommendations for software and hardware requirements including operating system considerations and hardware considerations. Some of these are discussed in *Chapter 1, Setting Up the Environment for Dynamics NAV*.
- Defining user access policies and Windows network access policies; these may be extendible to the Dynamics NAV security system as well.

These topics can be found in detail in Microsoft operating system documentation and other network-related documentation.

Security with SQL Server installation

The SQL security system is very robust and comprises the following two main components:

- **Access to the server**: This is the layer of security that involves granting access to the server using logins to authenticate the users and provide them with a secure connection to the server.

- **Access to the database**: This refers to the security defined by roles and permissions for appropriate database access to the users.

Dynamics NAV security models

There are two distinctive but not-so-different security models that build the security system for Dynamics NAV. They are mainly differentiated by how they synchronize the Dynamics NAV security system with the SQL Server security system and Windows security system. In the following table, we highlight the key differences between the two security models—Standard and Enhanced.

Synchronization	Standard Security Model	Enhanced Security Model
Speed of synchronization	Fast	Slow. The synchronization of all logins is slower with multiple companies.
Option to synchronize one login	No	Yes
Auto synchronize when logins are inserted, modified, or deleted in Dynamics NAV	Yes	No
Windows Users & Groups	Active Directory Windows groups and users + local groups	Only Active Directory Windows groups and users. Local groups are not displayed.
Windows Groups	Local domain Windows groups and from forest of domains(trusted domain).	Only Windows groups from local domain are displayed.
Required Extended Stored Procedure	xp_ndo_enumuserids	xp_ndo_enumusergroups

Switching between Enhanced and Standard security models

To change the security model from **Enhanced** to **Standard** or vice versa, we will have to alter the database, changing the **Security Model** option (on the **Advanced** tab). We need to make sure that the database is made as "single user only" (by clicking on the **Single User** checkbox on the **Alter Database** window). We must also synchronize all logins after the **Security Model** is changed.

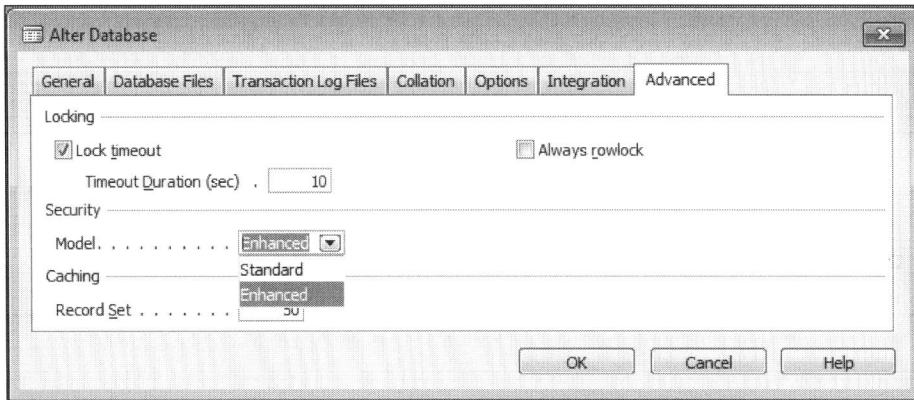

Why synchronize?

Synchronization is the process for the Dynamics NAV security system to match the SQL Server security system. This does not happen automatically and must be done manually after performing the following options:

- Applying a change to the objects in the database
- Changing the security model
- Making changes to the users, roles, and permissions in Dynamics NAV
- Restoring a backup
- Upgrading or converting the database and/or the client executables

Synchronizing one or multiple users

To synchronize one or multiple users, go to the **Windows Login** option under **Tools | Security**. Highlight the login(s) that need to be synchronized. Go to **Tools | Security | Synchronize Single Login** or **Synchronize All Logins**.

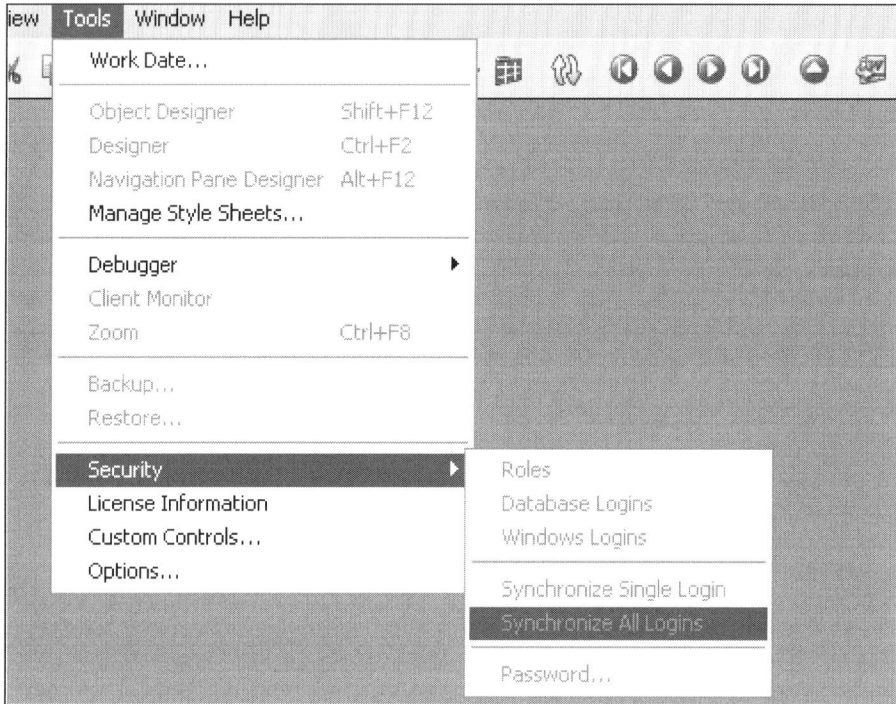

Users, logins, and passwords

The Dynamics NAV application provides two types of authentication methods to log in to the database, as explained next.

Creating database logins

These logins use database server (SQL or Classic) authentication to provide access to the application. We can create **Database Logins** as follows:

1. To create a database login in a Dynamics NAV Classic database server, go to **Database Logins** from **Tools | Security | Database Logins**.

2. Press *F3* to create a new **User ID** and **Name** for the **Database Logins**.

3. If we are using the SQL Server as the database for Dynamics NAV installation, we have to make sure that the database logins' **User ID** that we are using here also exists as a user on the SQL Server.

4. If we are using the Dynamics NAV Classic database server, we will have an additional column to specify the **Password** for the **User ID**.

The first user that we create should be the SUPER user (the user with super access to everything in the application). **SUPER** is one of the roles in Dynamics NAV that assigns all permissions (access to all forms, tables, reports, and other objects) to the user who has been assigned that role.

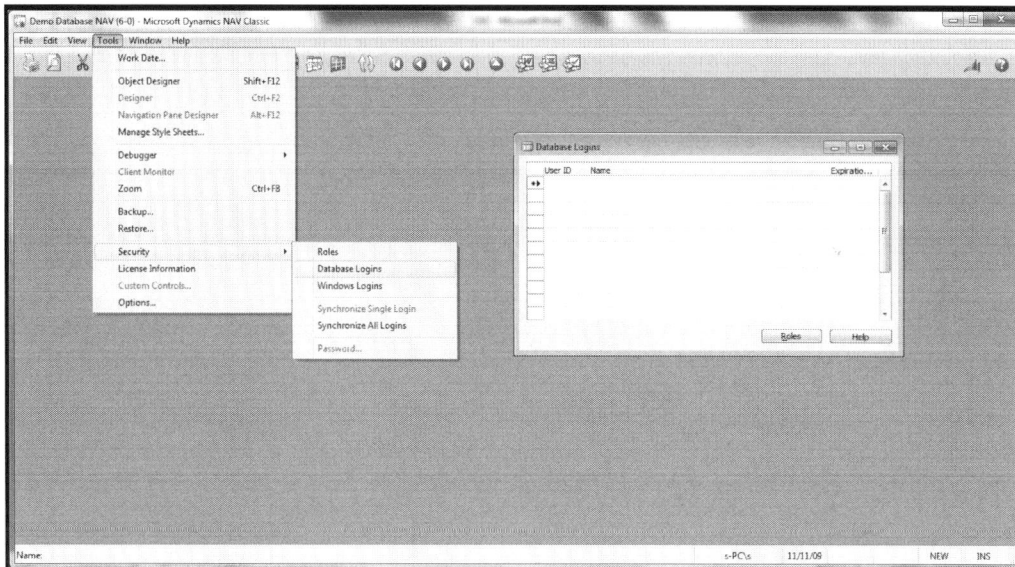

An **Expiration Date** can also be specified for the **Database Logins** in the last column on the right side of the **Database Logins** form. This **Expiration Date,** can be used, for example, by subcontractors or short term employees who need access to the Dynamics NAV application for only a given period of time.

Setting up user accounts

We can set up the users from the **User Setup** menu, in the **Administration** section, under **Application Setup** | **Users**.

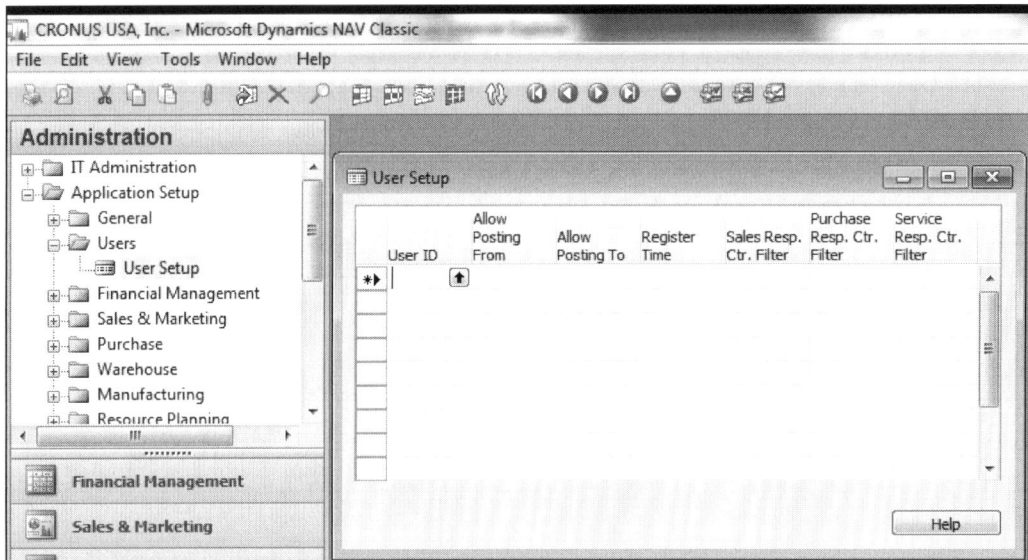

Using the **User Setup** screen, there is an option to control some basic features of the Dynamics NAV application.

We have the ability to restrict the date range of posts from the **Allow posting from** and **Allow posting to** fields; these fields take precedence over the posting date range specified in the **General Ledger Setup** form.

Users entering the system can also be restricted to particular responsibility center(s), thus allowing them to view/do transactions in that responsibility center only. There is also an option to restrict a database login to a particular company; this will be discussed in the *Roles* section later in this chapter.

There is an option to register the time for the users logging on to the system. If we mark the **Register Time** column for a user, the system will log the **User ID**, **Date** of login, and **Minutes** spent on the application. This will be updated every time the user logs off from the Dynamics NAV application.

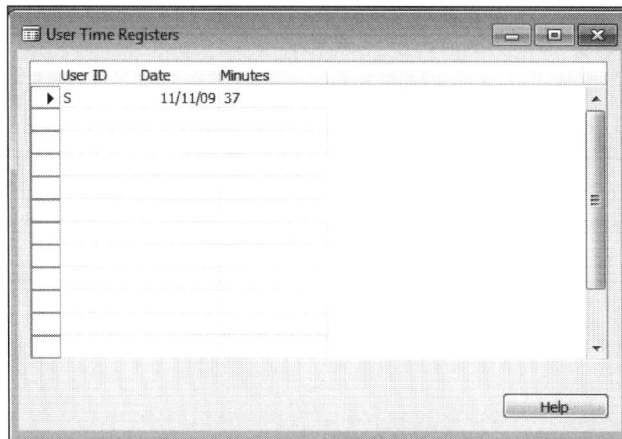

How is a USER ID used across the application

The **User ID** is tagged to almost every transaction and ledger entry, and helps in providing an audit trail for transactions.

Specific reports can be printed on separate printers by different users. This can be set up in the **Printer Selections** menu in the **Administration | IT Administration | General Setup | Printer Selections**.

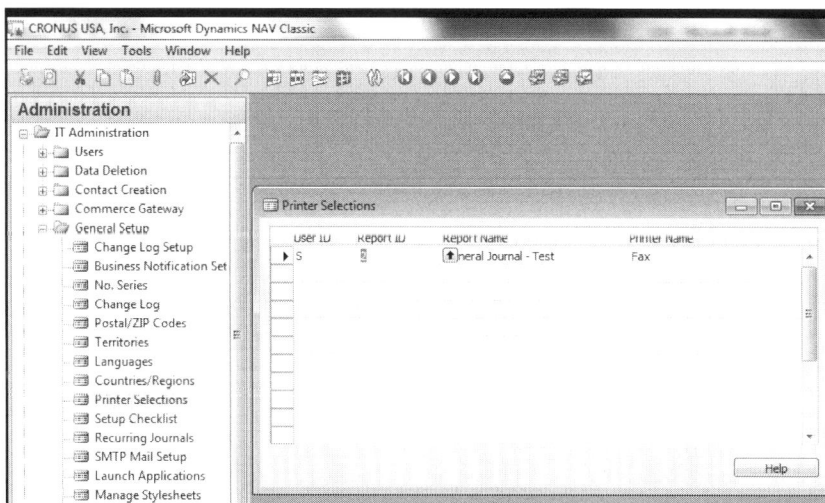

User ID(s) are also represented in the Change Log entries, if the **Change Log** option is enabled. For more information on the **Change Log** option, refer to the *Change Log* section in this chapter.

The creation of database logins, appropriate permissions, and so on can be done by a SUPER user or by a user who has appropriate permissions to change security for Dynamics NAV.

Logging in using Windows Authentication

Microsoft Windows operating system provides a robust and secure computing platform. Dynamics NAV is designed to leverage the Windows security system. The administrators have the ability to set up the Windows single sign-on feature with a Dynamics NAV installation.

When a user opens Dynamics NAV, they have the option to select **Windows Authentication**. If that is selected, we don't have to key in the username and **Password** while logging into the application, as shown in the following screenshot:

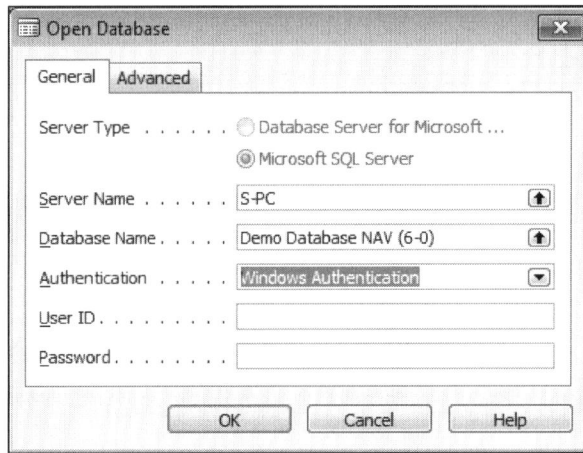

SQL extended stored procedures

To use the Windows Authentication with SQL Server option for Dynamics NAV, we need to add two extended stored procedures as follows:

- `xp_ndo_enumusersids.`
- `xp_ndo_enumusergroups.`

These two stored procedures come with the `xp_ndo.dll` file that comes along with the Dynamics NAV installation. The program will automatically add these extended stored procedures the first time Dynamics NAV connects to the server.

If we have already connected to the server, we will have to add these extended stored procedures manually. To add these stored procedures manually, follow the next steps:

1. From the `Product CD folder ..\SQL_ESP`, find `xp_ndo.exe`.

2. Run the file and enter the path to the `BINN` folder of the SQL Server installation. Make sure that the `xp_ndo.dll` is copied to this path.

3. Use Microsoft SQL Server Management Studio(2005) or Enterprise Manager (SQL 2000) to add extended stored procedures with the following names:

   ° `xp_ndo_enumusersids`

   ° `xp_ndo_enumusergroups`

4. Assign execute permissions for both the extended stored procedures to the public role in the SQL Server database.

Let's do a walkthrough of how to create Windows login(s) in the Dynamics NAV application, as follows:

1. While logged in to the database (as a SUPER user or user with permissions to create new users), go to **Tools | Security | Windows Logins**.

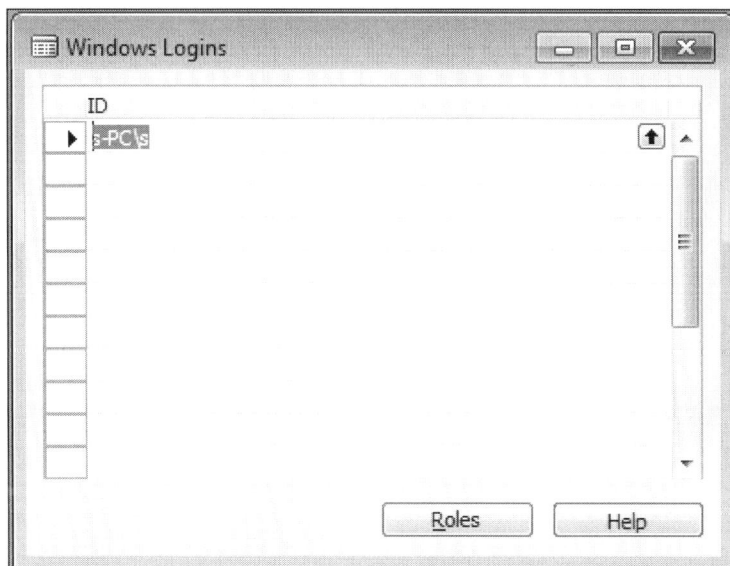

2. Press *F3* to create a new Windows login.

3. We can press *F6* or the **Assist Edit** button on the **ID** field to look up and select from among all the **Windows Users and Groups** available in the cluster of domains.

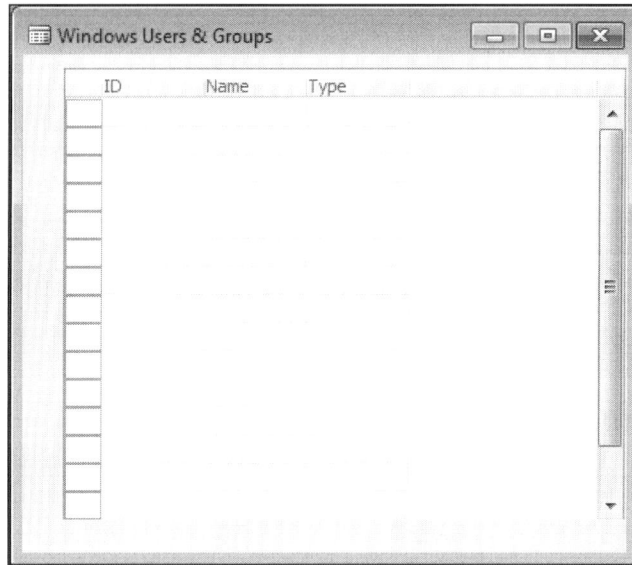

4. If we are using SQL Server as a database, after we have assigned the appropriate roles (for more information about assigning roles and permissions, go to the *Roles and permissions* section of this chapter) we will have to synchronize this new login with the SQL Server. To synchronize the Windows login to the SQL Server, go to **Tools | Security |Synchronize Single Login** or **Synchronize All Logins**. The synchronization will create the Windows login(s) in the SQL Server. More about synchronization is discussed earlier under the *Dynamics NAV security models* section.

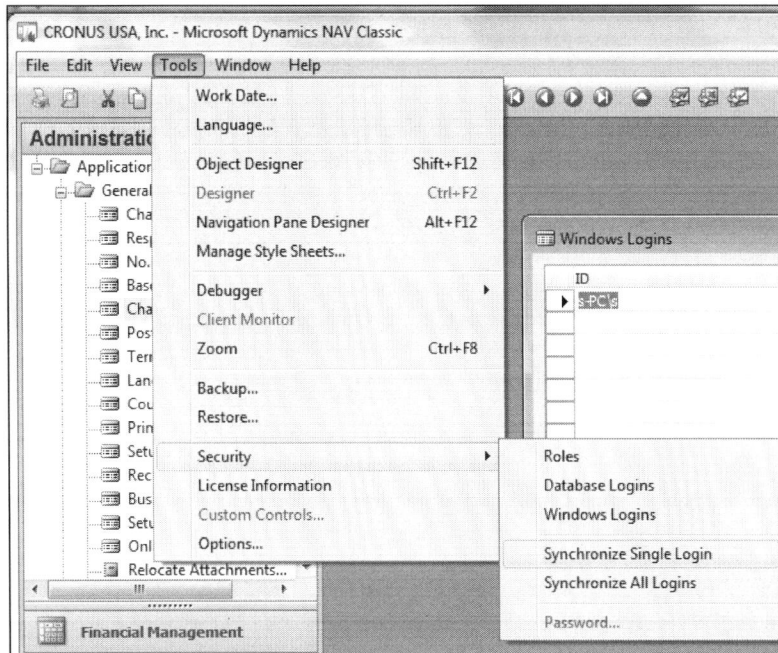

Why use Windows Logins?

Microsoft Dynamics security inherits all the extended security features of Active Directory, if **Windows Authentication** is used for accessing the Dynamics NAV application. It also makes the administration a lot easier and manageable.

Some of the biggest advantages of using Active Directory and **Windows Authentication** is that everything is manageable from within NAV (for database administrators). One of our favorite and highly recommended approaches is to use Windows groups. Using Active Directory Windows groups makes the setup of users and management of existing users almost effortless. Network administrators can just add the new Windows login to the appropriate groups when creating new users for the Dynamics NAV application.

Passwords

If we decide to use **Database Authentication** for our installation, we will have to specify passwords for all the database logins that we create.

To change the password for Dynamics NAV, go to **Tools | Security | Password**.

The following screenshot will prompt us to confirm our **Current Password** and then specify a **New Password** for the Dynamics NAV program (followed by a re-enter):

Roles and permissions

The Dynamics NAV security system provides extensive security and access control options to specify direct and indirect permissions for up to object-level (table-level) security and also record level security in the Dynamics NAV for SQL Server option. This layer of security, consisting of roles and permissions, is a very discreet layer of security on top of the SQL database security system and Windows security system.

There are no default users when we first start the database, either a new database or the demo database. The first login that we create—Windows or database login—must be a SUPER user, with access to the SUPER role in Dynamics NAV. This role has all the permissions for the application. We can add the SUPER user by adding a new user and assigning the **SUPER** role by clicking the **Roles** button at the bottom of the screen.

The SUPER user defined earlier can now create other logins and assign them roles according to the functions that users perform.

A **role** in Dynamics NAV is a set of permissions for various objects—tables, forms, Codeunits, reports or dataports, and so on.

It is highly recommended that before starting to assign and create new roles, we must take into account the standard Dynamics NAV roles that come along with the demo database. These are standard roles that provide a wide range of access control based on business functions.

Roles can be accessed from **Tools | Security | Roles**.

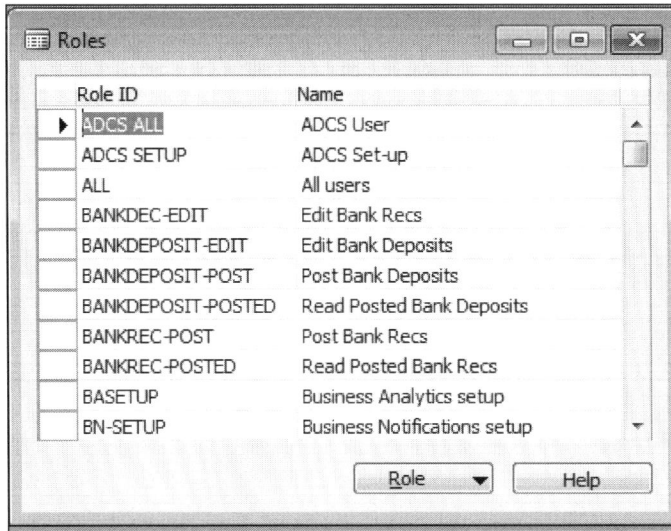

A database or Windows login can have multiple roles assigned to it. Let's assign roles to Windows or database logins as follows:

1. Open the **Database Logins** or **Windows Logins** window from **Tools | Security**.

2. Highlight or make sure our cursor is on the login that we want to assign roles to.

3. Click on the **Roles** button in the bottom.

4. Assign one or multiple roles in the screen that appears next. We can create a role by using *F3* and then looking up the list of roles by clicking **Assist Edit** (or press *F6*).

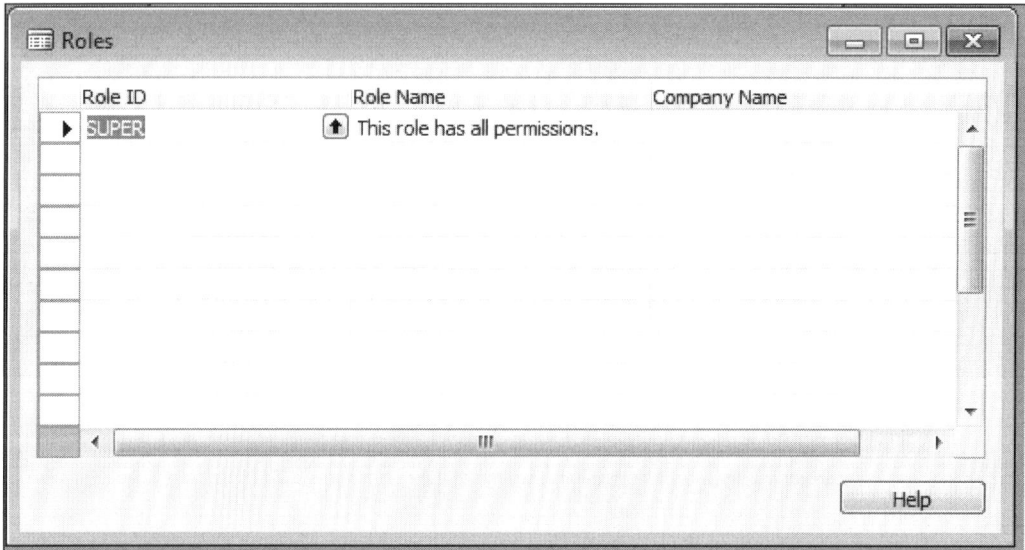

5. There is also an option to specify the **Company Name** on the right most column; this is used if we want to restrict a user to a particular company only.

Assigning permissions

Every role is a cluster of a set of permissions for various objects, which are as follows:

- **Table Data**
- **Table**
- **Form**
- **Report**
- **Codeunit**
- **XMLport**

- **MenuSuite**
- **System**
- **Page**

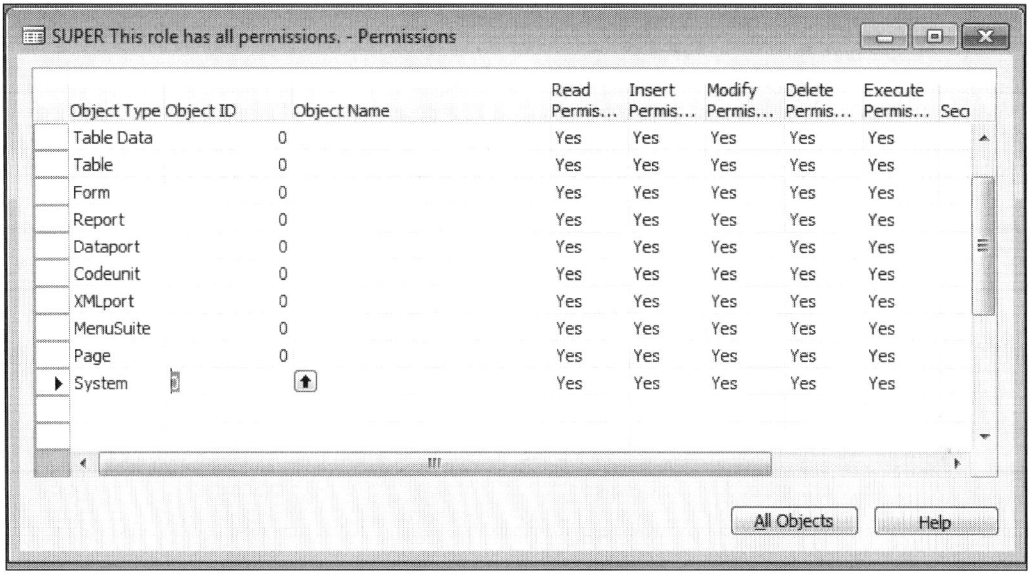

The previous screenshot shows the permissions assigned to the SUPER role in the Dynamics NAV demo database. The value **0** assigned to the **Object ID** field, indicates all objects of that object type will get included in the role, depending on the read, modify, execute, insert, and delete permissions.

While most of the previously given access to the respective objects in the database, the system object type is used to define a set of functions, which are not executed by the objects in the database, for example, importing and exporting object files.

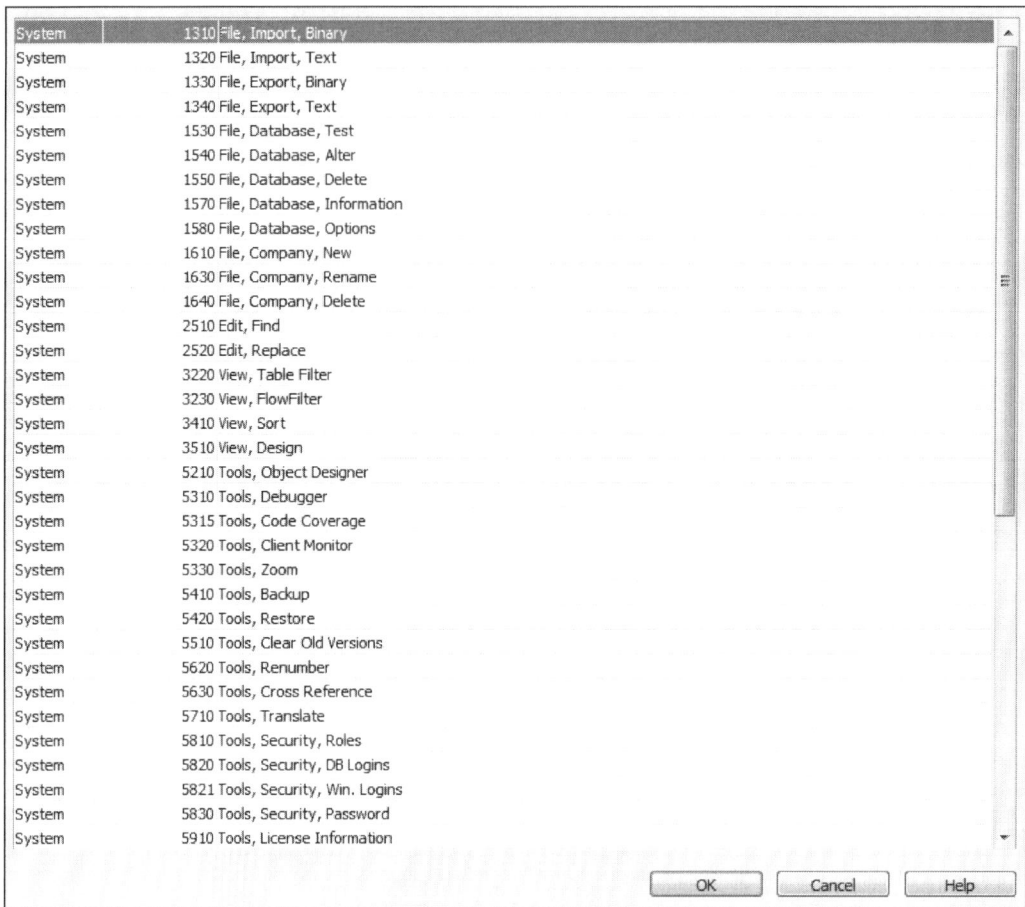

The **Permissions** field has three different options, as follows:

- **Blank**: No permissions are associated with this permission type (such as read, insert, modify, delete, or execute).

- **Yes**: The role has full permissions associated with this object.

- **Indirect**: This option gives access to the object through another object. For example, access to a table may be needed by a Codeunit that uses the table to either read from, write into, or modify the records. A lot of tables are modified by the `Codeunit 12 Gen. Jnl.-Post Line` and one of them is `Table 81- Gen. Jnl line`. Therefore, the user who has to perform posting, needs indirect access to the table (through Codeunit 12).

Creating a new user from scratch

Let's do a walkthrough of the process of creating a new user that needs access to read G/L Accounts. We will create from scratch the role(s) and the associated permissions with the role as follows:

1. Create a new database login (or could also be a Windows login) as shown in the next screen from **Tools | Security | Database/Windows Login**.

2. Go to **Tools | Security | Roles**.
3. Create a new role by using *F3*, named **COA (Chart of Accounts)** from General Ledger.

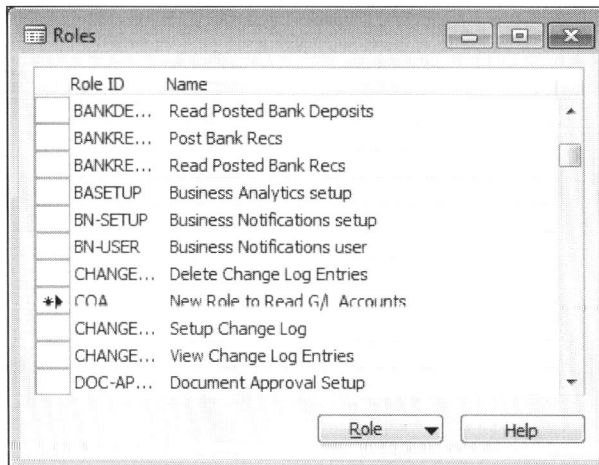

4. Click on the **Permissions** button from the **Role** menu button in the bottom of the form.

5. Assign appropriate permissions to the **Table Data-15 G/L Accounts**; in this case, we only need **Read Permission**.

6. We also need permissions for **G/L Entry** table, as there are flow fields in the **G/L Account** table that read from the **G/L Entry** table.

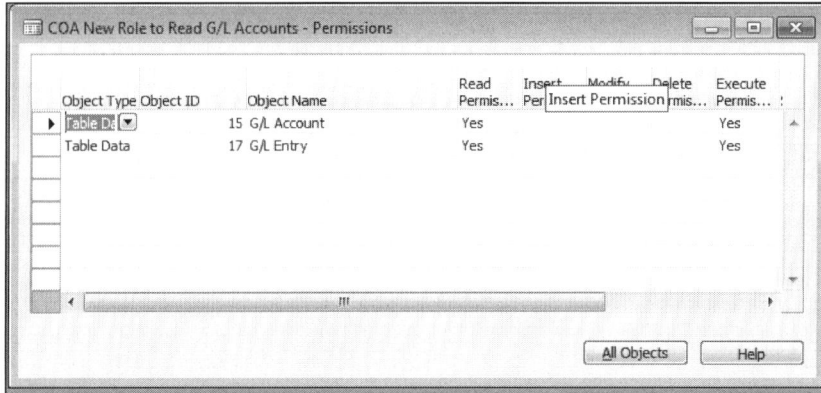

7. Let's go back to our **Database Logins** window and assign the appropriate roles to our new user. In addition to the new role we previously created, we also need to add an **ALL** role to the user's list of roles. This role is kind of a prerequisite for any other roles (except **SUPER**). This contains access to basic tables, forms, and other objects that are needed for proper functioning and start up of the Dynamics NAV application.

8. The next process is to synchronize our new user (if we are using SQL database); we could either use **Tools | Security | Synchronize one Login** or **Synchronize All Logins** to synchronize the new user and associated roles.

Security filter—record-level security

Security filters—record level security/access control can be explained by extending the previously described example for accessing **G/L Accounts**. Let's take an example where we want the user to view only balance sheet G/L Accounts.

To accomplish the record-level security, we use security filters from the **Permissions** window. Click on the **Assist Edit** button in the **Security Filters** field in the **Permissions** window and select the field on which we want to apply filters.

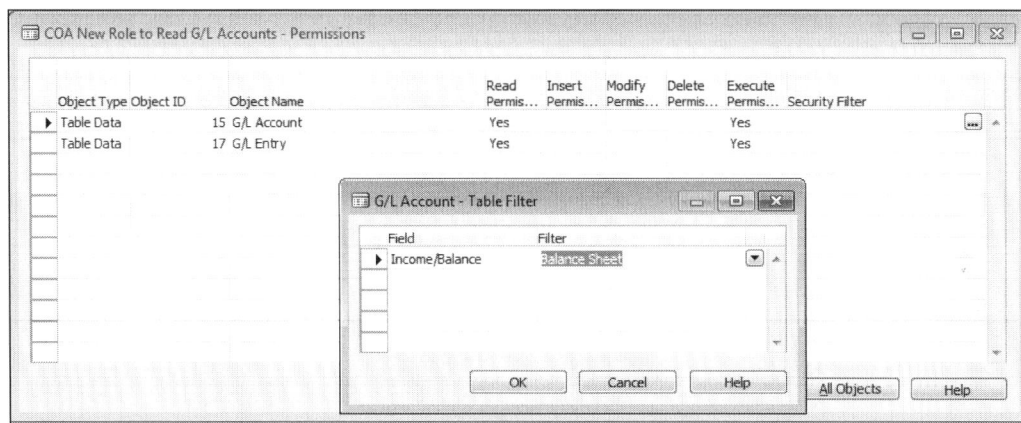

Record-level security is available only if we are using the SQL database.

Sarbanes Oxley compliance

The **Sarbanes Oxley compliance** or **SOX compliance** has been a huge concern for corporations across North America over the last few years. We will discuss some of the features and practices in Dynamics NAV that help make the life of SOX-compliance auditors a lot easier.

Security, backups, and authorization

Dynamics NAV provides an extensive range of tools to work with security, most of which have been discussed in this chapter. In addition, Dynamics NAV also provides an integrated security structure with Windows Authentication and the SQL Server security model. The Dynamics NAV backup feature provides the ability to back up the database from within the application. Regular backups could also be scheduled to ensure effective database recovery procedures are in place.

Access control and audit trail

In addition to that, a user is restricted by Dynamics NAV roles and permissions to the level where the user is able to perform his daily activities on the system. This is further cemented with the new Role Centers in Dynamics NAV RoleTailored Clients.

In the SQL Server option for Dynamics NAV, it is possible to provide record-level security, which ensures that specific users view only specific areas of the application.

The **User ID** of the user performing a transaction in Dynamics NAV is tagged at every stage, including data entry in the documents and journals. The **User ID** can also be found in the ledger entries and on posted documents, thus enabling a smooth trail of transactions supported by dates and times.

Shown next is a screenshot of the **G/L Entries**, showing **User ID** and **Source Code** to identify the source of transactions:

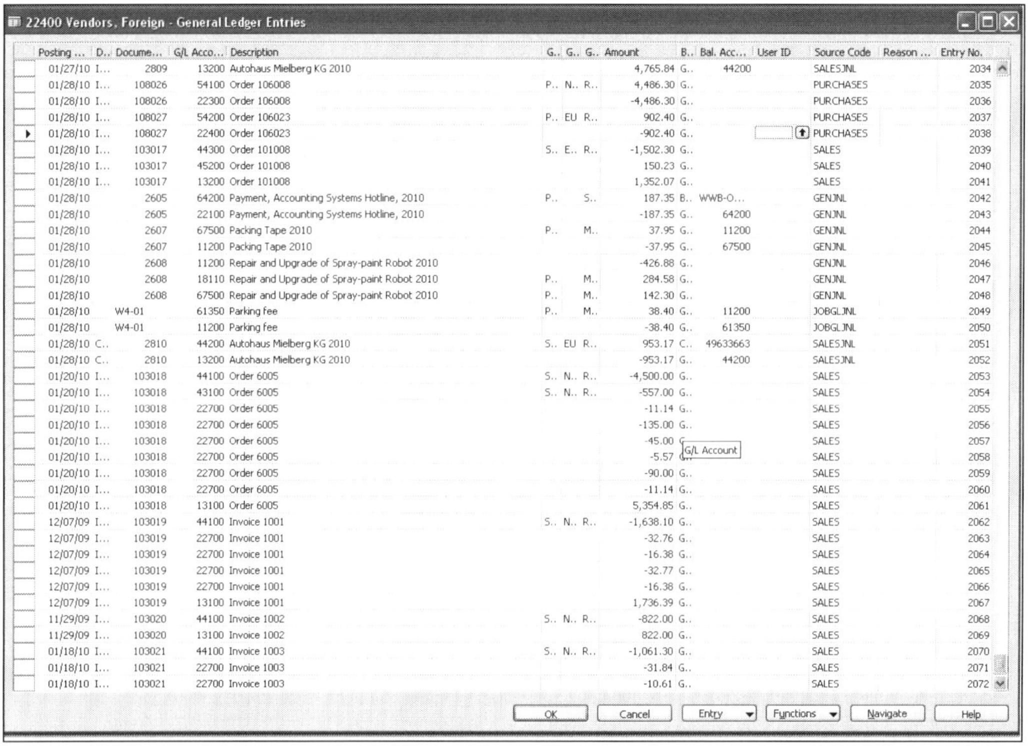

Change Log

A Change Log feature in Dynamics NAV, if set up, provides a log of all the changes made to the data, including insert, modify, or delete.

To set up the **Change Log** in Dynamics NAV, let's follow the next steps:

1. From the **Administration** menu in Dynamics NAV, scroll to the **Application Setup** and then expand further to **General** and open the **Change Log Setup** screen as shown next:

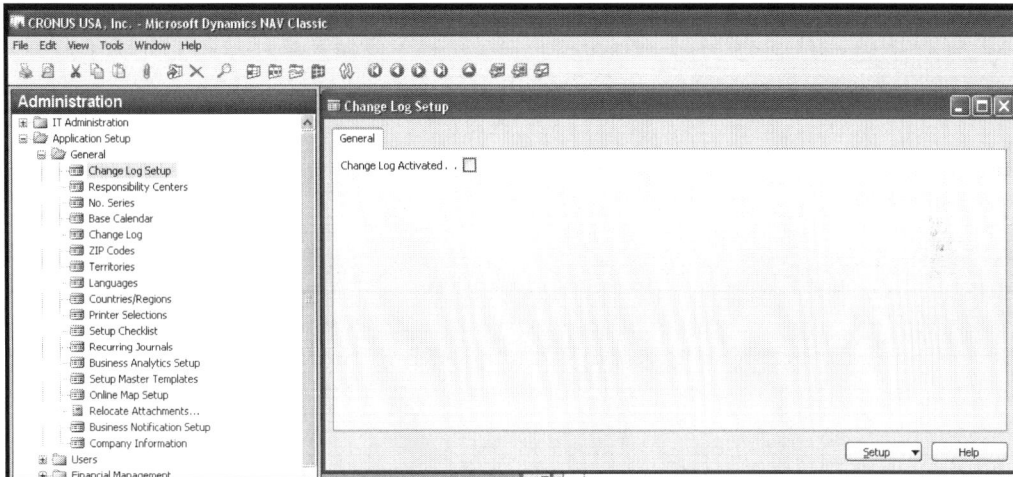

2. To start using the **Change Log**, check the **Change Log Activated** checkbox.

3. Click on the **Setup** menu button at the bottom of the screen and select **Tables**.

4. This opens a list of all Dynamics NAV application tables, with options to log insertions, deletion, or modification of those tables, as shown next:

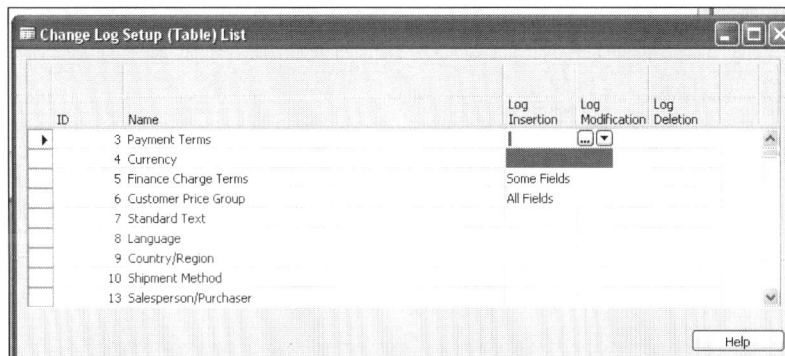

5. For each table, that needs to be change logged, there is an option to select all fields in the table, or select a collection of some fields (by selecting some fields and clicking the **Assist Edit** button).

6. Once the setup has been done, the changes in the application tables start getting logged in the **Change Log Entries** screen as shown next:

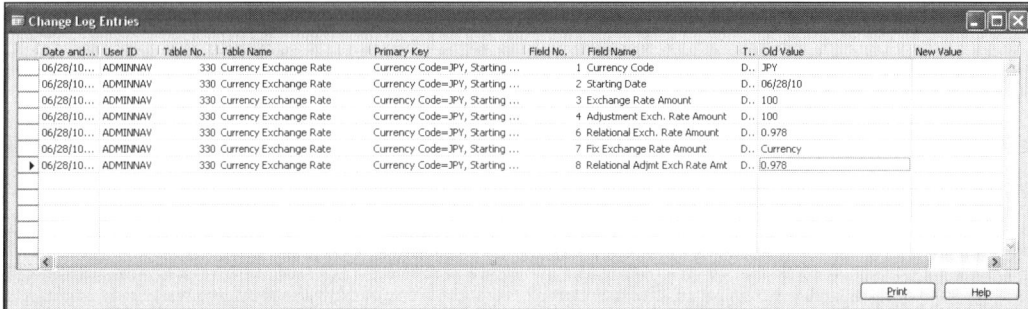

Data validation and accuracy

The Dynamics NAV application provides several checks and balances at every step throughout the various stages of application including data entry and postings. Language-specific error messages and prompts assist users with the data accuracy and ensuring the correct information enters the application. There are checks to ensure the debits and credits match; field-level controls are established throughout the application to ensure the fields that are mandatory for the transaction are entered by the user before moving on.

Effective change management

Change management procedures are an essential part of maintaining a SOX-compliant application. A few aspects of change management to keep in mind while defining the organization's change management policy are as follows:

- Every change must be driven by a business case or an issue raised by a business process owner. This must be documented.

- The change done to the application must be tested in a separate test database before releasing the code to a live database.

- The object files must be logged and so should be the objects changed to accomplish the change.

- Proper versioning of objects ensures the previously defined measures are accomplished easily.

- Appropriate approvals must be given to promote the object changes to the database and must be documented in the change management process.

There are several tools available across a wide range of partners to manage the code promoted to the database and report on it.

Summary

This chapter talks about the security, roles, permissions, and other related topics for the Dynamics NAV application. Microsoft has ensured that Dynamics NAV is a very secure application for enterprises and the chapter outlines some features of the application that ensure security across various application areas.

5
Backing up and Restoring a Dynamics NAV Database

In this chapter, we will focus on an area that is critical for any application, especially when the organization's financial data are involved.

Having some sort of backup strategy is indispensible to any organization. Though there are different ways to build up one, we will highlight a few different aspects in this chapter. A backup strategy for the organization must have the ability to restore and recover all the data entered into or modified in the database, ideally up to the point of failure.

Creating and restoring backups using a Dynamics NAV client

Creating a backup using a Dynamics NAV client is one of the easiest methods of backing up and restoring the database.

Retrieving a backup of the Dynamics NAV database

We can use the following steps to retrieve a backup of the Dynamics NAV database (SQL Server database or Classic database):

1. After connecting to the appropriate Dynamics NAV database go to the **Tools** menu and click on **Backup**.

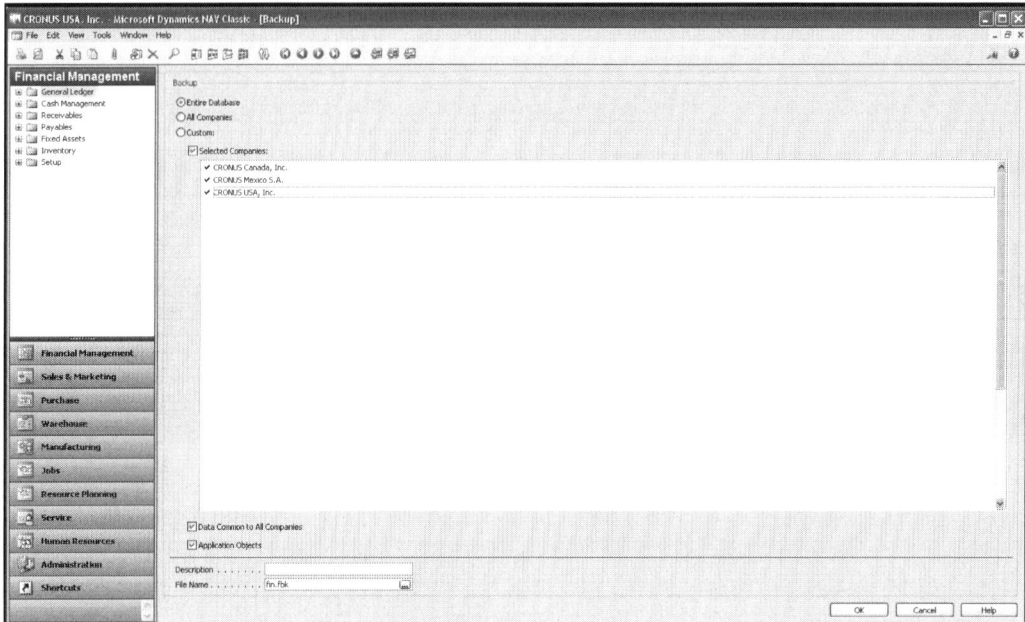

2. Select one of the following **Backup** options:
   - ○ **Entire Database**: This backup is used to back up all the three main components of the Dynamics NAV database backup, as follows:
     - • **Selected companies**: Select from the list of companies in the database that need to be backed up. Full backup selects all companies by default.
     - • **Data common to all companies**: This option includes backing up the data that is common to all companies and includes the data such as login information, permissions, roles, printer selections for the Dynamics NAV client, and so on.
     - • **Application Objects**: Selecting this option will also include all Dynamics NAV objects in the backup file.
   - ○ **All Companies**: All the companies in the database are selected by default when we use this option.
   - ○ **Custom**: Any of the three options—**Selected companies**, **Data Common to All Companies**, or **Application Objects**—can be selected.

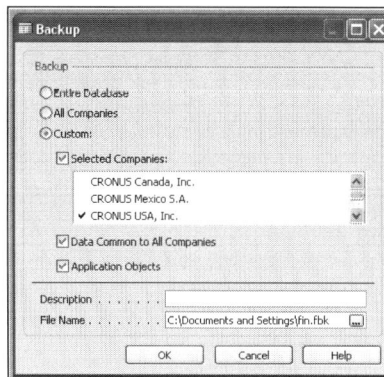

If the backup is too large to be stored over one file, the system will create multiple files incrementing the filename with the number. The backup process file is compressed and a database test is run on the database before the backup is complete.

Restoring the database

To restore the database, a blank database has to be created first, either in the SQL Server or Classic database server. Then follow the next steps to restore the database:

1. While logged in to the database, click **Tools | Restore**.

2. Select the backup file (.fbk).

3. A window similar to the **Backup** window appears, where we have to select from the available options of **Selected Companies**, **Data Common to All Companies**, and **Application Objects**.

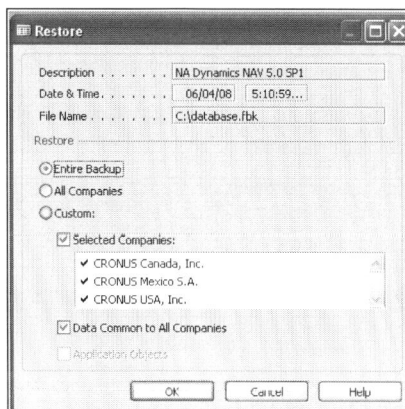

Handling error messages

An error message generated during the restore process could possibly be due to one of the following reasons:

- If the database size of the blank database is not enough to restore the backup into the database. This will not occur in the Dynamics NAV client for SQL Server, if the data and log files are set to unlimited growth. Please refer to the *Expanding the database* section of this chapter to find out how to expand the database.

- If we have a linked object in the backup, the SQL components required by the linked objects need to exist in the SQL database prior to the restore process. This is only applicable while backing up using the Dynamics NAV SQL Server option.

- If the datatype of a field in the blank database differs from what is in the backup file. This also affects some properties of the field; if a property of the field such as the length of the field is different and smaller (40 characters) in the database and the backup is trying to restore the field value of 50 characters.

- If there is another company in the database, which has the same name as the company that is being restored from the backup file.

- If there are checksum issues/corrupt backup files.

- An error may be generated during the synchronization process if the Windows login table ID(s) and Windows logins do not match. Synchronization automatically starts after the restore process. If this error occurs, the restore will not roll back, and the synchronization will have to be manually done after fixing the login issue. This is applicable only while backing up using the Dynamics NAV SQL Server option.

- If there is a character in the restore data that is not in the current SQL collation.

- If a lowercase character is found in a CODE field (if entered directly in SQL).

- If a date issue is caused by differing regional settings.

Using HotCopy backup

The HotCopy backup utility can be used to take a backup of the Microsoft Dynamics NAV database from the server location onto the hard drives.

We can use the following command prompt parameters to run `HotCopy` from the command prompt. Alternatively, we can also put these command-line parameters in a source file and provide that as a single parameter:

Parameter	Description	Example

Source	Specify the path of the database, name of the database, and name of the database file (if the file is in the same folder as `HotCopy.exe`). We can specify multiple files as the source if we need to back up multiple databases.	`HotCopy source = c:\program files\ Microsoft Dynamics NAV\..database.fdb.`
		
		`HotCopy source=database.fdb.`
		
		(This will use the `database.fdb` from the `HotCopy` folder).

Destination	Specify the path of the directory where the database file needs to be copied. If there is already a backup in the directory, it will be overwritten by HotCopy.	`HotCopy source = c:\.. Destination = \\Backupserver\ NAVBackups\.`
Dbtest	This is the option to run the database test on the NAV Classic database before it is backed up. This corresponds to the **File | Database | Test** option. The three options are **minimum, maximum,** and **normal**.	`HotCopy source = c:\..Destination = \\Backupserver\ NAVBackups\ dbtest = maximum.`
CC	This parameter is used to specify if a consistency check needs to be performed on the backup. This check performs a bit-by-bit comparison of the original database with the backup taken.	`HotCopy source = c:\.. Destination = \\Backupserver\ NAVBackups\ dbtest = maximum CC= yes.`
Description	Use this parameter to give a description of the backup.	`HotCopy source = c:\..Destination = \\Backupserver\ NAVBackups\ dbtest=maximum CC= yes.`

Parameter	Description	Example
Servername	This is the name of the Dynamics NAV Classic database server. The default is local host.	HotCopy source = c:\..Destination = \\Backupserver\ NAVBackups\ dbtest=normal CC= yes servername = NAV2009
Osauthentication	We can use this parameter if we intend to use Windows Authentication. The only option is either "yes" or specify the username and password as defined in the subsequent parameters.	Hotcopy source = c:\..Destination = \\Backupserver\ NAVBackups\ dbtest=normal CC= yesServername = NAV2009 Osauthentication = yes
User	Enter the username for the user creating the backup, if Windows authentication is not used.	
Password	Enter the password for the user creating the backup, if Windows authentication is not used.	
Nettype	Specify the network type used between database server and clients. The options are **netb** for NetBIOS, **tcps** for TCPS, and **tcp** for tcp/ip.	

HotCopy creates an exact snapshot of the database files in the specified destination folder. To restore the database backup created using HotCopy, copy the backed up files (.fdb) to the database folder and restart the database server.

Testing the database

Running periodic tests on the Dynamics NAV database must essentially be a part of the organization's periodic database management plan.

The backup process in Dynamics NAV has a built-in basic database test, which runs during the backup process.

To run a database test on the Dynamics NAV database, go to **File** | **Database** | **Test**.

Starting the test

The following options can be selected before starting the test:

- **Minimum**: This is the test that the Dynamics NAV backup process automatically initiates. This includes testing primary keys and data, and also testing all BLOB fields in the database. When run, this test validates the data in the primary keys, which is readable and sorted appropriately, and all the BLOB fields in the database can be read.

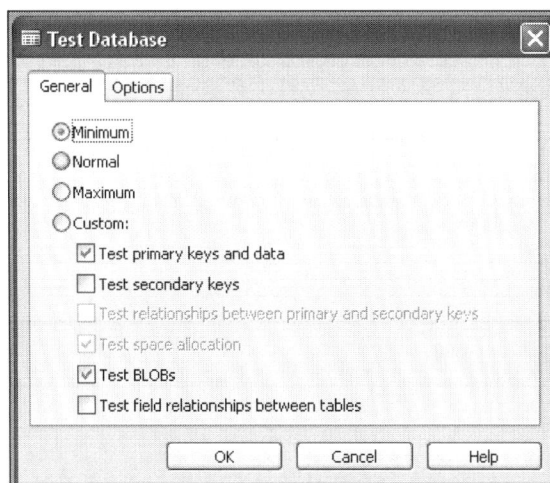

- **Normal**: In addition to the checks done in the **Minimum** DB tests, this test also checks for secondary keys and space allocation.

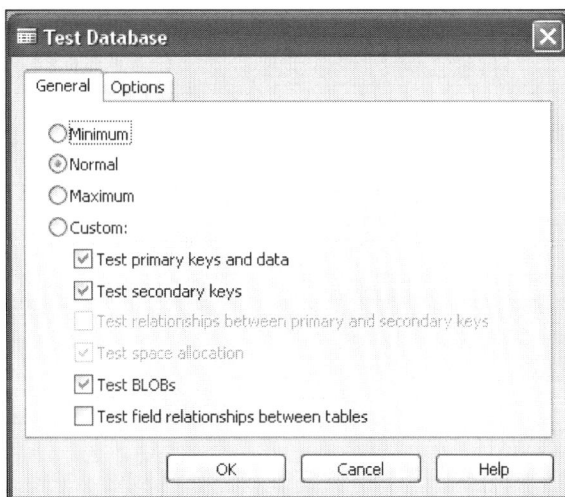

- **Maximum**: This test includes testing for field relationships in addition to the tests available in **Normal**.

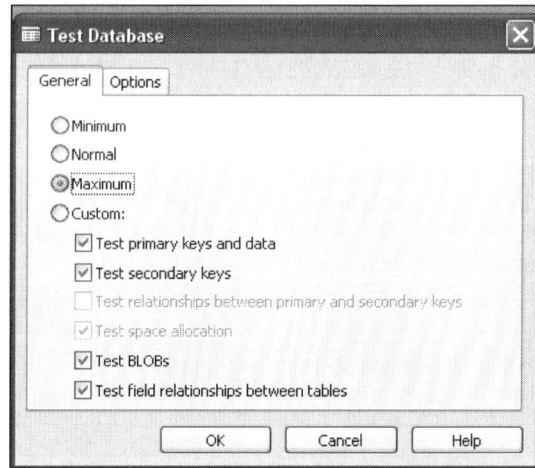

- **Custom**: This feature allows us to configure a test by selecting any of the tests from the list.

On the SQL Server database, most of these tests involve running the SQL Server **Database Consistency Checker (DBCC)**.

Viewing the output of the database

Output of the database can be viewed using the following different options, which can be selected from the **Options** tab of the **Test Database** window:

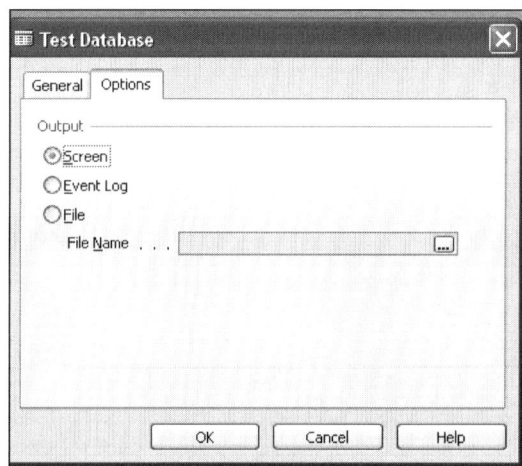

- **Screen**: Selecting this option would pop up error messages during the running of the database test. User intervention will be needed to continue the test beyond the displayed error message.

- **Event Log**: This option, if selected, would display the error messages in the event log of the server.

- **File**: This option will output all error messages in a text file. The location of the text file must be specified in the **File Name** field below this option.

Backing up and restoring with SQL Server

If we are using the Dynamics NAV SQL Server option, the recovery plan for our backups will depend a lot on the recovery model we have selected for the database.

We can change/select the recovery model for the Dynamics NAV SQL database either from the SQL Server management studio, or from the **Alter Database** window in the Dynamics NAV application, as shown in the following screenshot:

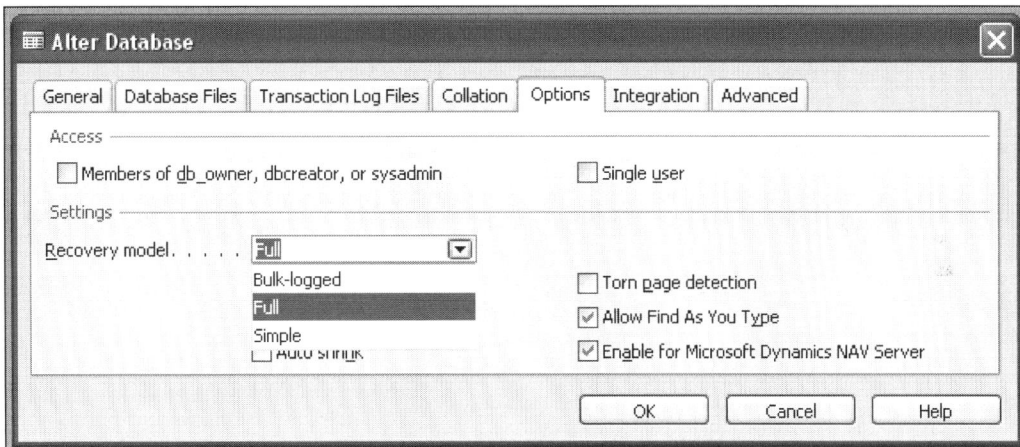

We have the following options for the **Recovery model**:

- **Bulk-logged**: The transaction log will contain information only about the large transactions. This model provides support against disk failure and does not affect the performance as much as the **Full** mode does.

- **Full**: The advantage that full log has over all other models is that it guarantees the recovery of the database to the point of failure. It is advisable to use this method for production databases, provided the resources are available to do so. It is the most flexible method for recovery and takes the most transaction log space, and using this method, the last committed transaction can also be recovered.

- **Simple**: This is the easiest and the least resource-hungry of all recovery types. The recovery of the database is limited to the last backup taken. It is recommended to be used for development databases or non-production databases, where recovery of data is not critical.

The client backup for SQL Server option remains the same as it is in the C/SIDE or Classic version of Dynamics NAV.

SQL Server gives a lot of flexibility in terms of database backup, restore options, and the options for backup media (such as tapes, drives, or other backup devices). It also provides the ability to overwrite backups and perform incremental/ differential backups. Generally, SQL backup can be done while transactions are being done on the database.

Creating a server-side SQL backup

Let's walk through the process of creating a server-side backup of the Dynamics NAV database as follows:

1. Go to **SQL Server Management Studio** and from the **Object Explorer**, highlight the Dynamics NAV database, as shown in the following screenshot:

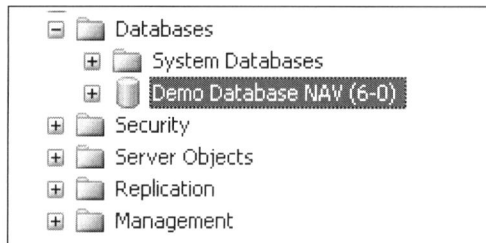

2. Right-click on the database and navigate to the **Back Up...** menu, as shown in the following screenshot:

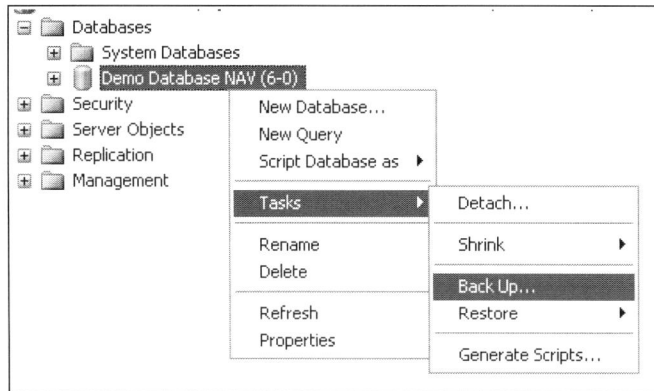

3. Select **Full** in **Backup type**, and add a name for the backup and an appropriate description.

4. Click on the **Add** button and select the **Disk** option under **Destination** and input the filename and name of the directory in the **File name** field under **Destinations on disk**, where we would want to store the backup.

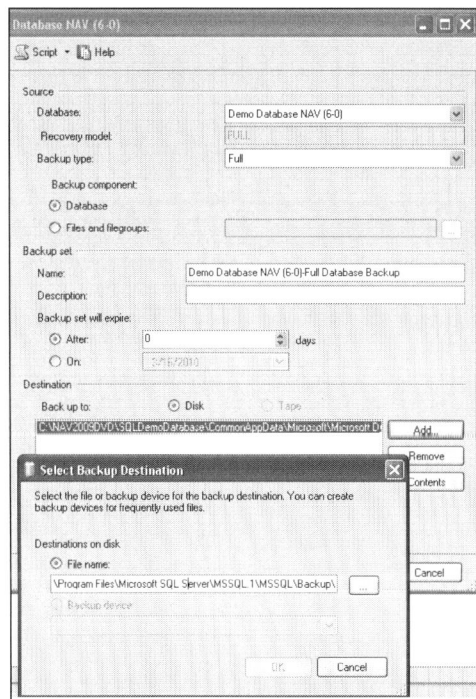

5. A message similar to the following screenshot is displayed after the backup is successfully completed:

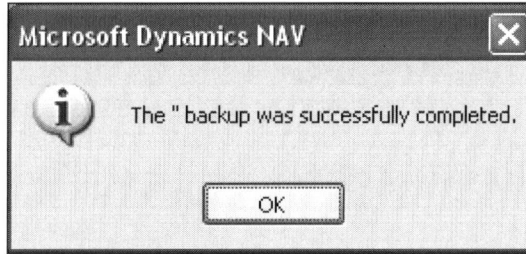

Restoring the SQL backup

Let's walk through the process of restoring the SQL backup as follows:

1. To restore the SQL backup, right-click on the **Database(s)** item on the SQL Server and click **Restore**.

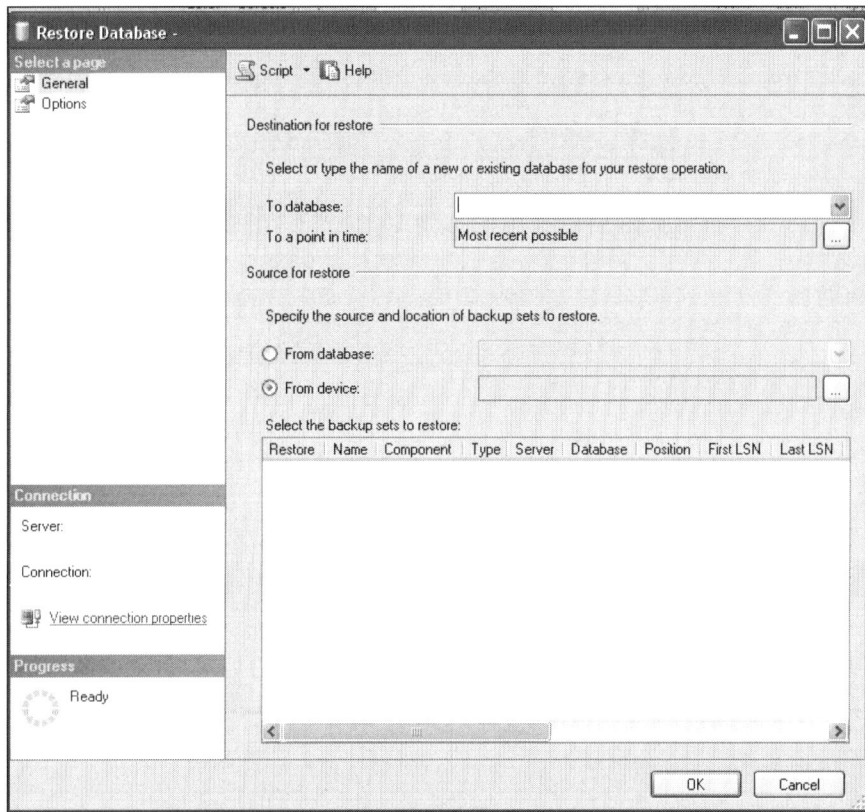

2. Enter the name of the new or existing database in the **To database** field.

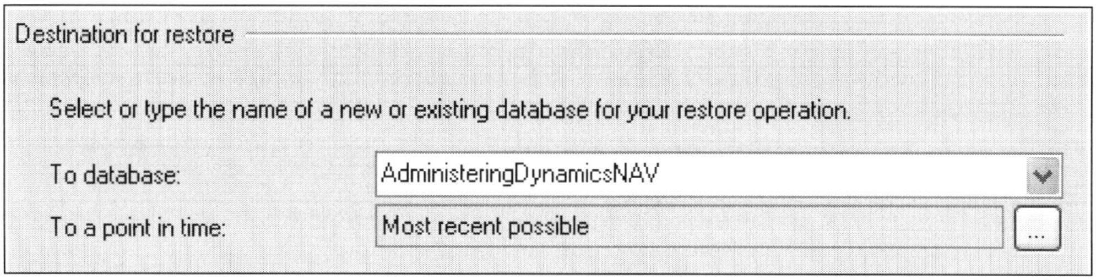

Destination for restore

Select or type the name of a new or existing database for your restore operation.

To database: AdministeringDynamicsNAV

To a point in time: Most recent possible

3. In the **Source for restore**, select the **From device** option.

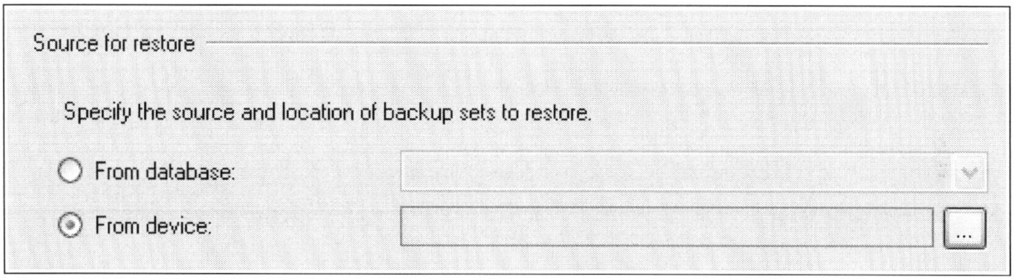

Source for restore

Specify the source and location of backup sets to restore.

○ From database:

◉ From device:

4. To select the backup files created in the previous backup process, click on the **Assist Edit** button in the **From device** field.

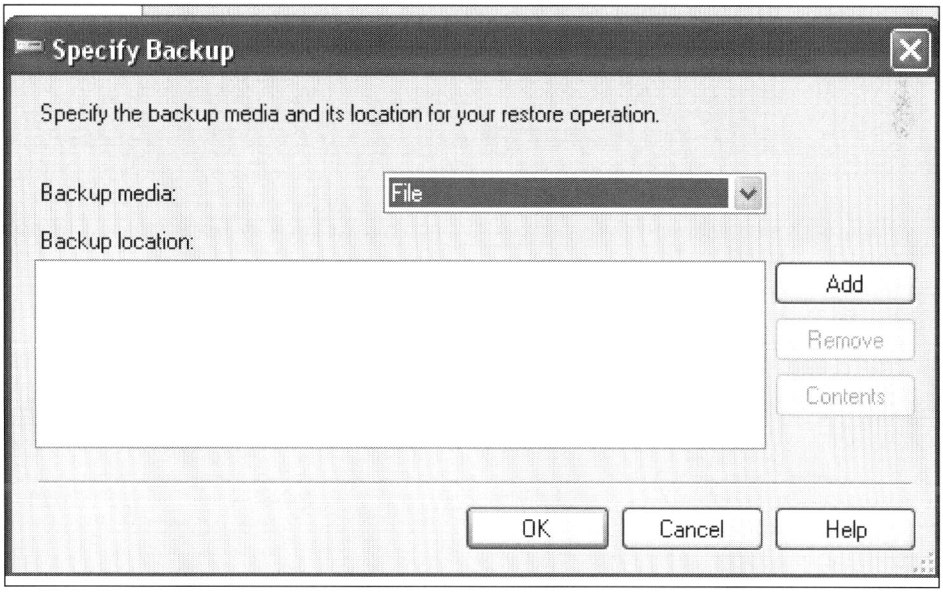

Specify Backup

Specify the backup media and its location for your restore operation.

Backup media: File

Backup location:

Add

Remove

Contents

OK   Cancel   Help

5. Then click **Add** and select the backup file from the location on the drive.

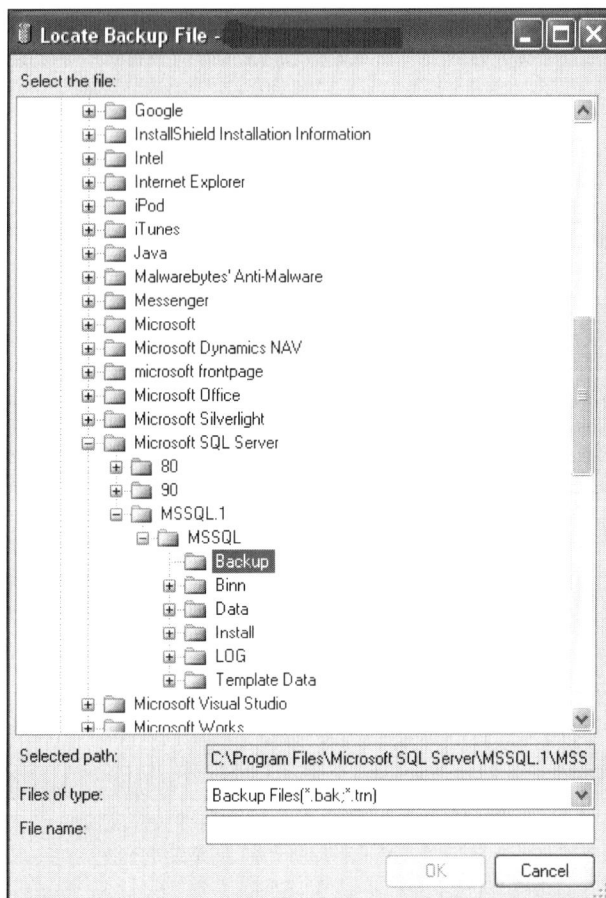

There are some key differences between the SQL Server backup and the backup done by using the Dynamics NAV client.

The ability to back up specific Dynamics NAV companies is one of them. The ability to update only data (not the application objects) is also a key differentiator available in the Dynamics NAV client-based backup.

SQL Server on the other hand supports transaction log backup, file/file group backup to back up individual files, and differential backups, apart from the standard full database backup. As a SQL Server backup is server-based, it is faster than the Dynamics NAV client-based backup.

For more detailed information on using SQL backups, it is recommended to review the documentation for Microsoft SQL Server.

Synchronizing a SQL database

Synchronization is a process to ensure that a SQL database security system is synchronized with that of Dynamics NAV. As discussed in the previous chapter, it is important to synchronize the database after restoring of the database is complete.

It is imperative to synchronize the security model after the restore of the backup has been completed successfully, for both Enhanced and Standard synchronize models.

Expanding the database

While SQL database files can be set to auto expand up to a certain limit. We have to manually expand a Dynamics NAV Classic database. The restore process can fail with an error if there is not enough space in the database to restore.

To expand the Dynamics NAV Classic database, let's follow these steps:

1. Go to **File | Database | Expand...** as shown in the following screenshot:

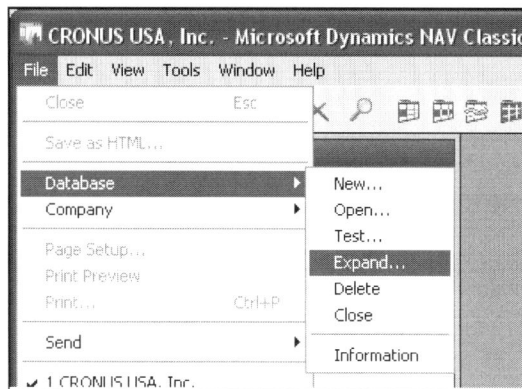

2. The **Expand Database** window appears as shown in the following screenshot:

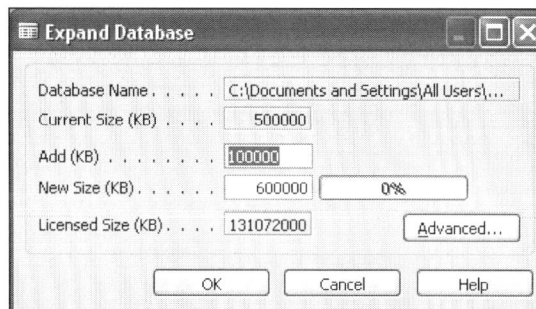

3. Enter the size that we want to expand by in the **Add (KB)** field of the window or enter the desired database size in the **New Size (KB)** field of the window.

4. If we click on the **Advanced...** button of the **Expand Database** window, there is an option to add multiple database files while expanding the size of the database. We can add multiple files to the existing database. That way, we can spread the database across multiple files.

5. The **Expand Database(Advanced)** window appears as shown in the following screenshot:

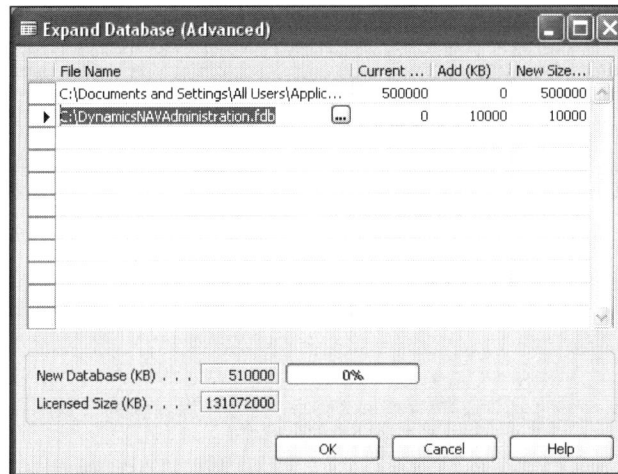

6. To monitor the size of the added files, go to **File | Database | Information** and the following window appears:

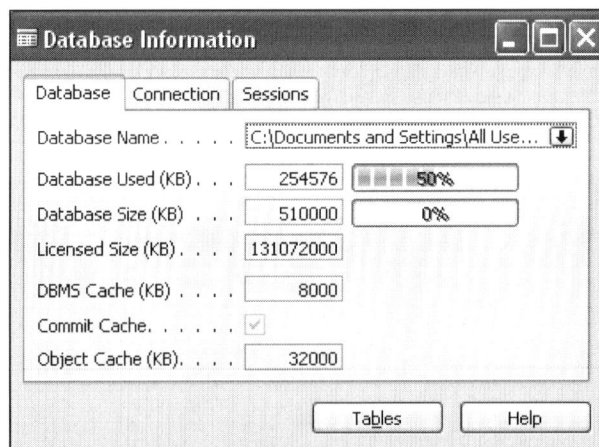

7. Click on the drop-down for the **Database Name** field to open the **Database Files** window, as shown in the following screenshot:

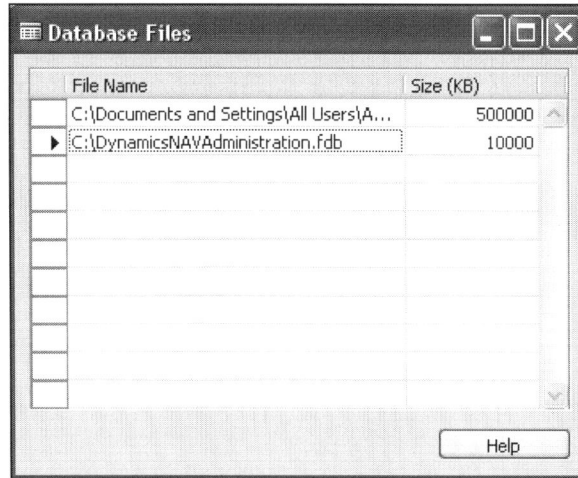

File Name	Size (KB)
C:\Documents and Settings\All Users\A...	500000
C:\DynamicsNAVAdministration.fdb	10000

Database Files

Things to consider while defining the backup strategy

The following are the considerations for defining a backup strategy:

- Prepare a disaster recovery plan for the organization.
- Consider doing a backup before any major development code promotion to the database, deleting, modifying, optimizing, and expanding the database.
- Select the appropriate SQL database recovery model.
- Plan to include all possible failures, including a complete loss of the physical server and/or media failure.
- System databases of SQL Server should also be backed up.
- A quarterly check of the restore of the backup to make sure the backups are not corrupt.
- The backup location must be physically different from our data location.
- A daily backup of the complete database is ideal. In the case of larger databases with lots of transactions, a differential/incremental backup can suffice.
- Also, back up the transaction log if using SQL Server for Microsoft Dynamics NAV.

Summary

We first created a backup and restored it using a Dynamics NAV client. We also looked at how to handle error messages encountered while restoring. We then took a backup of the Microsoft Dynamics NAV database using the HotCopy utility and analyzed its parameters. We tested the backup and then we also created a backup in SQL database and restored it. Then we saw how we can expand the database and monitor its size. Finally, we looked at the considerations for defining the backup strategy.

6
Performance Tuning

A significant number of companies are now considering and using the SQL Server option for Dynamics NAV. As their databases expand, the NAV experts are experiencing a surge in the number of requests for fine-tuning the database performance of Microsoft Dynamics NAV. While it's easy to get into the programming and technical part, we've tried to focus more on the administration part and how a few things can make a huge impact on the performance of the database. This includes some of the following activities and how to do them properly while using the Microsoft Dynamics NAV with SQL Server option:

- Configuring and setting up a Microsoft SQL Server database for Microsoft Dynamics NAV
- Writing customized applications and code efficiently for the Microsoft Dynamics NAV for Microsoft SQL Server database option
- Periodically tuning and monitoring the performance of the SQL Server database

To cover these options in this chapter, we highlight some of the most commonly used methods and procedures. Some of the topics that are being specified in this chapter will be of great help in performance troubleshooting and would surely assist in prevention and diagnosis to rectification of any foreseeable performance troubles.

Configuring a SQL Server database for Microsoft Dynamics NAV

It is imperative that while configuring Microsoft Dynamics NAV, the hardware and software recommendations from Microsoft are taken into consideration. From using the latest version of Microsoft Windows, Microsoft SQL Server, or other Microsoft stack products that are intended to be used with Dynamics NAV or the hardware/server sizing, it is important that the Microsoft guidelines for these are taken into account. Some of these software/hardware sizing requirements are mentioned in *Chapter 1, Setting Up the Environment for Dynamics NAV*.

Let's discuss some of the parameters and features that are to be properly set at the time of setting up the Dynamics NAV database on the SQL Server.

Defining database and transaction log files

While defining the **Database Files** and **Transaction Log Files** of the Dynamics NAV SQL server database, it is strongly recommended to store the two sets on two separate physical drives. This not only helps greatly in improved performance of the database, but is also a key feature of a better disaster recovery management plan.

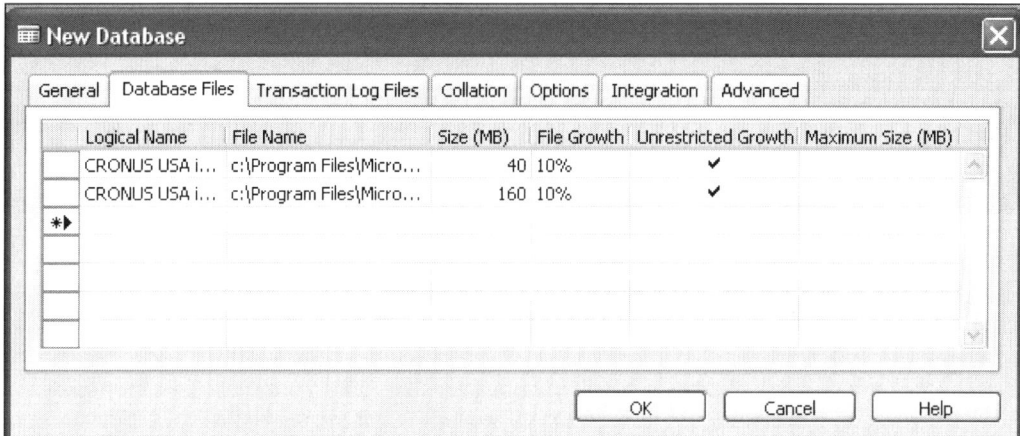

In order to avoid manually increasing the size of the database files every time it reaches the brink, we could check the **Unrestricted Growth** option for the database and log files. This can also be achieved by using the ALTER DATABASE T-SQL command on the SQL Server after the database has been created. The only disadvantage is that, this feature of unrestricted growth uses a lot of system resources and we will have to monitor the disk size for the database and log files.

Defining rules using collations

Collations are used to define the rules for a particular language, character set, or region. In SQL Server, the collation can be defined at various levels. The various objects of an SQL Server instance inherit the collation type from instance, though that can be changed later on for each database, column, variable, or parameter. In the Microsoft Dynamics NAV SQL Server database option, collation can be specified under the **Collation** tab while creating the database or by using the **Alter Database** option under the **Collation** tab.

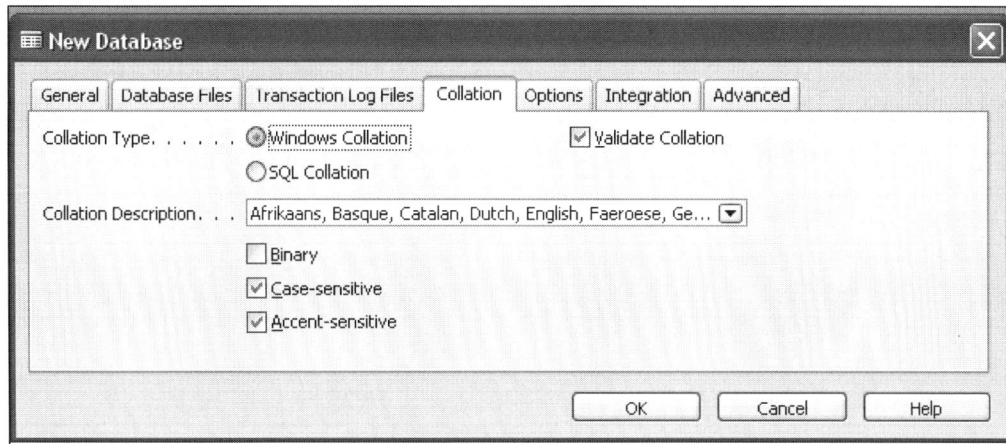

Binary is case sensitive and is the fastest sort order. However, it cannot be used concurrently with **Case-sensitive** and **Accent-sensitive** options.

Writing less expensive C/AL code for customizations

There are a few considerations to keep in mind while writing a customized C/AL code, as poorly written code can affect the performance of the application or a business process significantly.

Retrieving data using FINDFIRST/FINDLAST/FINDSET

Using FINDFIRST instead of the following FIND('-') statement is also an inexpensive command to retrieve the first record from the recordset.

The following is the code for retrieving the first record using the FIND statement:

```
GLEntry.SETRANGE(...);
IF NOT GLEntry.FIND('-') THEN
  MESSAGE('No entries in the GL Entry table');
```

The previous code can be replaced with the following code:

```
GLEntry.SETRANGE(...);
IF NOT GLEntry.FINDFIRST THEN
  MESSAGE('No entries in the GL Entry table');
```

Using FINDLAST instead of the following FIND('+') is an inexpensive way to retrieve the last record from the recordset.

The following is the code for retrieving the last record using the FIND('+') statement:

```
GLEntry.SETRANGE(...);
IF GLEntry.FIND('+') THEN
  MESSAGE('Last entry no. used -'+ GLEntry."Entry No.");
```

The previous code can be replaced with the following code:

```
GLEntry.SETRANGE(...);
IF GLEntry.FINDLAST THEN
  MESSAGE('Last entry no. used -'+ GLEntry."Entry No.");
```

> FINDFIRST and FINDLAST should not be used with the REPEAT UNTIL or NEXT command, as these two commands do not create a cursor to the next record, which is needed in the loop.

Instead of using the loop statements with FIND('-') command, use the inexpensive statement FINDSET to find the subset of records in the recordset.

The following is the code for retrieving the subset of records using the FIND('-') statement:

```
IF GLEntry.FIND('-') THEN
  REPEATUNTIL GLEntry.NEXT = 0;
```

The previous code can be replaced with the following code:

```
IF GLEntry.FINDSET THEN
  REPEAT UNTIL GLEntry.NEXT = 0;
```

Using the NEXT statement

The use of the NEXT statement inadequately could be the source of the biggest performance glitches. The interpretation of NEXT by SQL has to be explicitly defined if a NEXT is used without finding a subset, with FINDFIRST or FINDLAST, or is used after a changed key/filter.

Using ISEmpty

Instead of using IF Recordset.FIND('-') THEN using IF Recordset.ISEMPTY THEN is more efficient and less taxing on the server resources.

Locking the recordset

While programming on the Dynamics NAV for SQL Server option, it is a good practice to use LOCKTABLE and lock the recordset before modifying any records. This ensures that the uncommitted dataset that is read from SQL Server is locked and cannot be modified by another user.

Locking occurs when the following sequence of events takes place:

1. User X reads a record without using locktable.
2. User Y reads the same record without locks.
3. User Y modifies the record.
4. User X gets the error message **Another user has modified the record for this tablename after you retrieved it from the database**.

If both users X and Y in the previous example use explicit locks before fetching the record, they are blocked and will have to wait, until one or the other releases the lock.

> **Deadlocks** can occur if both the users are blocking each other and both of them are waiting for either one of them to release the lock or resources.

Let's take a look at the following example:

1. User X locks the customer, vendor table.
2. User Y locks the customer, vendor table.
3. User X gets the customer 10000 and User Y gets vendor 10000.
4. User X tries to get vendor 10000, User Y tries to get customer 10000.
5. User X gets a deadlock warning, while user Y is able to get the desired record. SQL Server randomly decides which user can get the record.

To avoid the previously mentioned conditions, we'll use the following guidelines at least whenever possible:

- Don't use "message" statements or any other user input mechanism after the table has been locked.
- Perform validations prior to the locking of table.

Disabling the "find-as-you-type" feature

The "find-as-you-type" feature in Dynamics NAV takes a heavy toll on performance, as with every keystroke, the SQL query is done.

Fine-tuning the SQL Server database for Dynamics NAV

Before we discuss about fine-tuning the performance of the database for Dynamics NAV, it is important to discuss some key features of the Dynamics NAV application that comprise the core architecture of the application, and the majority of performance issues could be attributed to improper use or misuse of these features.

SIFT

In the Classic database server option, **SIFT (Sum Index Flow Technology)** is used to make the calculation of balances, sums, and so on. In any other database, this is normally done through calculations and could be a time-consuming process if there are thousands of records in the table. The SIFT data is stored in indexes, which are also called secondary keys in the Classic database server option. The balances based on the "secondary keys" are stored in separate indexes in the database. The programmer can define which fields need calculation by defining the **SumIndexFields** for the keys, as represented in the following screenshot. Therefore, the retrieval time for things such as account balances and such others is minimal, making the application extremely fast:

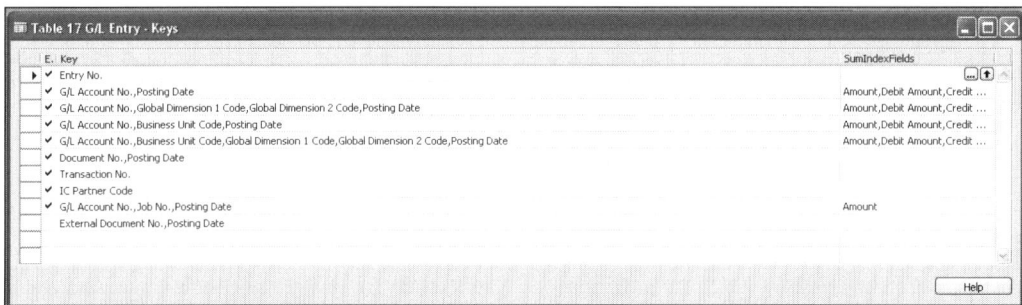

What gives a boost to SIFT is the ability to filter on the underlying values that make up SIFT balances. This technology is also known as the **flow filter technology**, which complements the basic SIFT technology in a significant way.

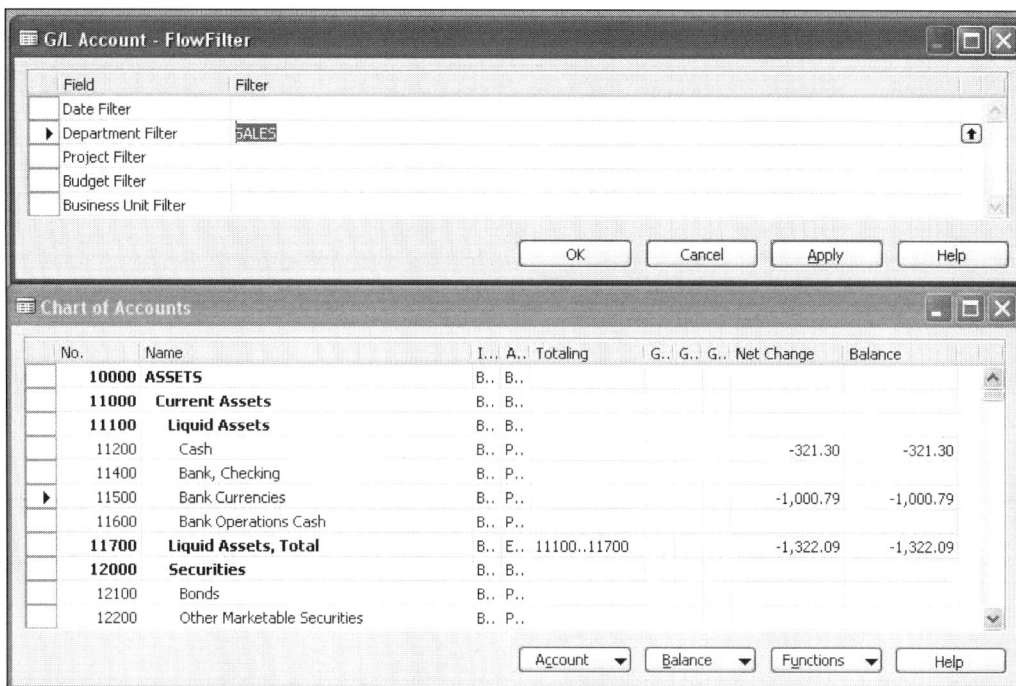

When SIFT was initially implemented on the Microsoft SQL Server database option for Dynamics NAV, it was done by storing these SIFT columns in summarized tables called **SIFT tables** that were continuously updated through SQL triggers. Thus, the procedure was expensive and took a toll on the performance when a table containing SIFT indexes was updated.

From the Dynamics NAV 5.0 Service Pack 1 version, Microsoft decided to use indexed views in SQL Server instead of SIFT tables. Dynamics NAV creates one SQL indexed view per key, regardless of how many sum indexed fields there are in that key. Having too many SIFT indexes can adversely affect the performance of the application.

> Having too many fields in the SIFT indexes is also not advisable.

The `MaintainSIFTIndex` property of the index in the base table could be used to optimally design the SIFT indexes. If there is the possibility of the base table not growing so rapidly, it is recommended to keep the `MaintainSIFTIndex` property to **No**.

For more information about SQL indexed views, we can refer to the *Microsoft SQL library*.

Using indexes/keys in Dynamics NAV

Maintaining indexes for Microsoft Dynamics NAV has also been seen as a big performance issue. This is one of the major reasons for performance issues in the Dynamics NAV Classic database. The Microsoft SQL Server is clever enough to sort the data without any index, if the dataset being sorted is not huge.

To access these properties of the keys, go to **Object Designer**, highlight the table in which the key needs to be modified, click on **Design** to open the list of fields in the table, and go to **View | Keys**. A window similar to the following screenshot opens, showing the list of keys:

To open the properties of a particular key, highlight the key and then click on **View | Properties**, as shown in the following screenshot:

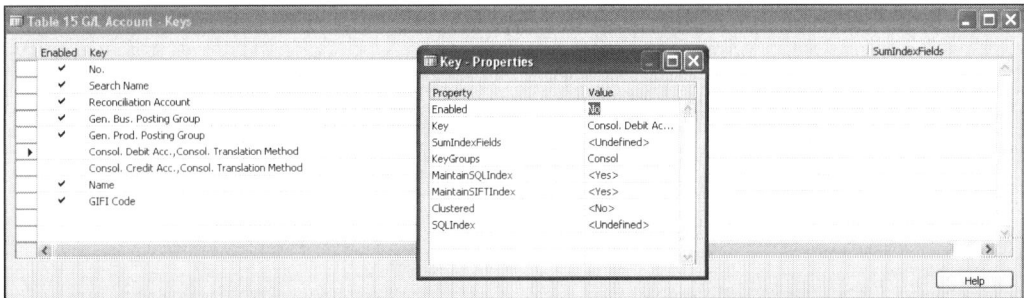

These indexes or keys could be used optimally by using the following properties of the keys:

- **Enabled**: This is a property to enable or disable an individual key. A lot of times, developers create a one-off key to be used in a particular report or another piece of customization. This one-off key can be disabled or enabled based on the utilization or frequency of the use of customization.

- **SumIndexFields**: This property is used to define the `SumIndexFields` (whose sum needs to be maintained in the SQL indexed views). A maximum of 20 `SumIndexedFields` can be selected.

- **KeyGroups**: This is a method of combining the various keys together so that they could be enabled or disabled together.

  For example, in the following screenshot we see that the, **Key Group** property is defined as **Consol**, which is one of the key groups in the database.

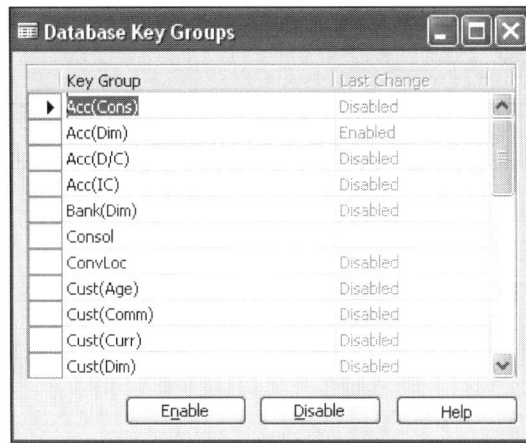

  Keys can be combined together based on the nature of the use of keys or a particular application area.

  To enable or disable a key group, go to **File | Database | Information**. Click on the **Key Group** button in the bottom of the **Database Information** form to open a list of key groups defined in the database.

- **MaintainSQLIndex**: Microsoft SQL Server is clever enough to sort the data without an index, though to have the SQL Server sort faster, an index of the fields to be sorted can be created. Any writes to the table will be slower, as the number of indexes in a table grows, as those indexes will have to be updated along with each write transaction.

- **MaintainSIFTIndex**: As discussed in the previous section of this chapter, we need to set this property to **No** if the data to be maintained in the SIFT base tables is less.

- **Clustered**: This is where we define whether or not the index is clustered. Clustered indexes are used to specify the sorting of data as it pertains to the storage in the table.

> In Dynamics NAV and also in a SQL Server database, a primary key is a clustered index by default.

- **SQLIndex**: We can specify here the actual list of fields that need to be a part of the SQL index.

Investigating the performance of the database

There are a few key performance troubleshooting techniques that are effective in identifying the bottlenecks in the performance of the database.

Updating statistics

There are several tools available from various Microsoft Dynamics ISV(s) that provide effective tools for monitoring the performance of a Dynamics NAV database. We will limit ourselves to the SQL Resource Kit provided by Microsoft in this section of the chapter.

The Index Defrag tool

The **Index Defrag** tool is a Dynamics NAV tool that comes along with the Microsoft Dynamics NAV SQL Resource Kit, and helps in identification of the keys that need to be defragmented:

1. Look for the `index defrag tool.fob` file in the Dynamics NAV SQL resource toolkit. Import the object file into the database and run the **50090** form, **Index Defrag Card**.

2. Start with filling the setup form from the **Defrag** menu in the bottom as shown in the following screenshot:

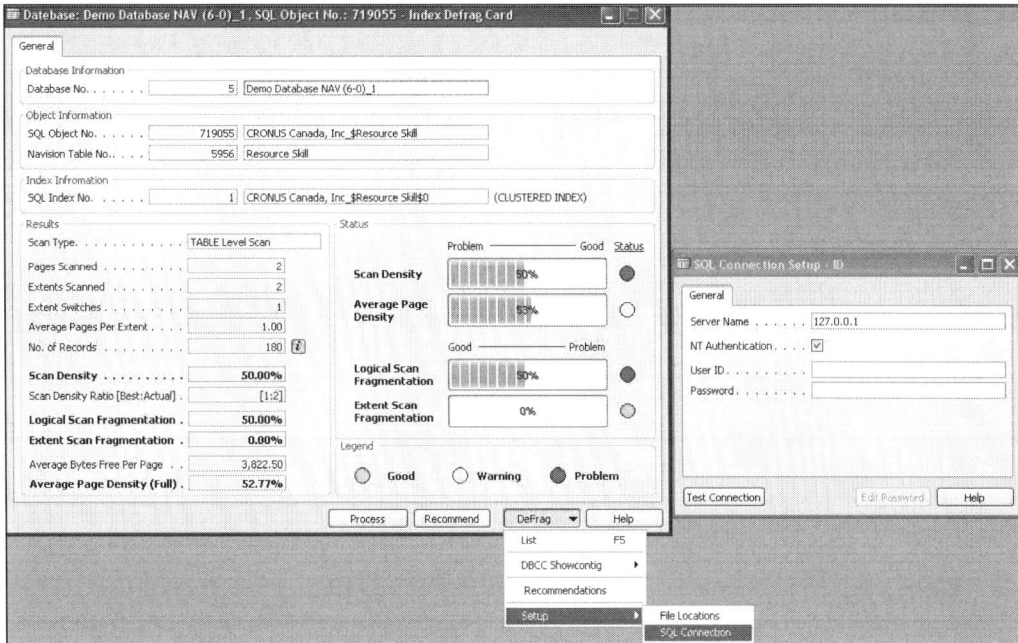

3. Once we have set up and tested the connection to the SQL Server, the next step is to specify the file locations for the scripts that this tool would generate. Specify that in the **File Locations Card**.

4. On the **Execute** tab on the **File Locations** form, specify the isqlw.exe filename and the path of the file for the SQL Server, if it is not on the same machine.

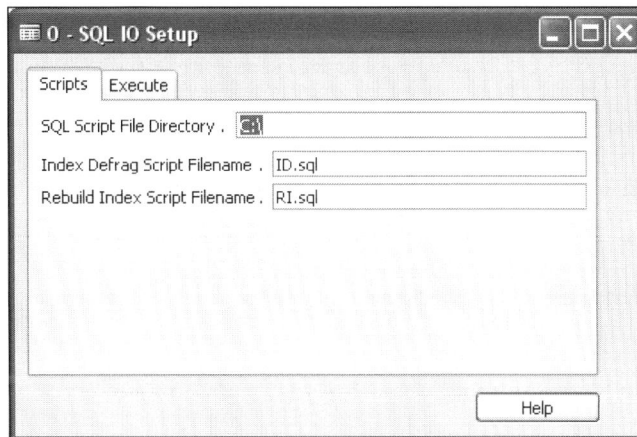

5. The tool runs **DBCC ShowContig** in the background when we click on the **Process** button on the form, and gathers information about various indexes and also more information about fragmented indexes.

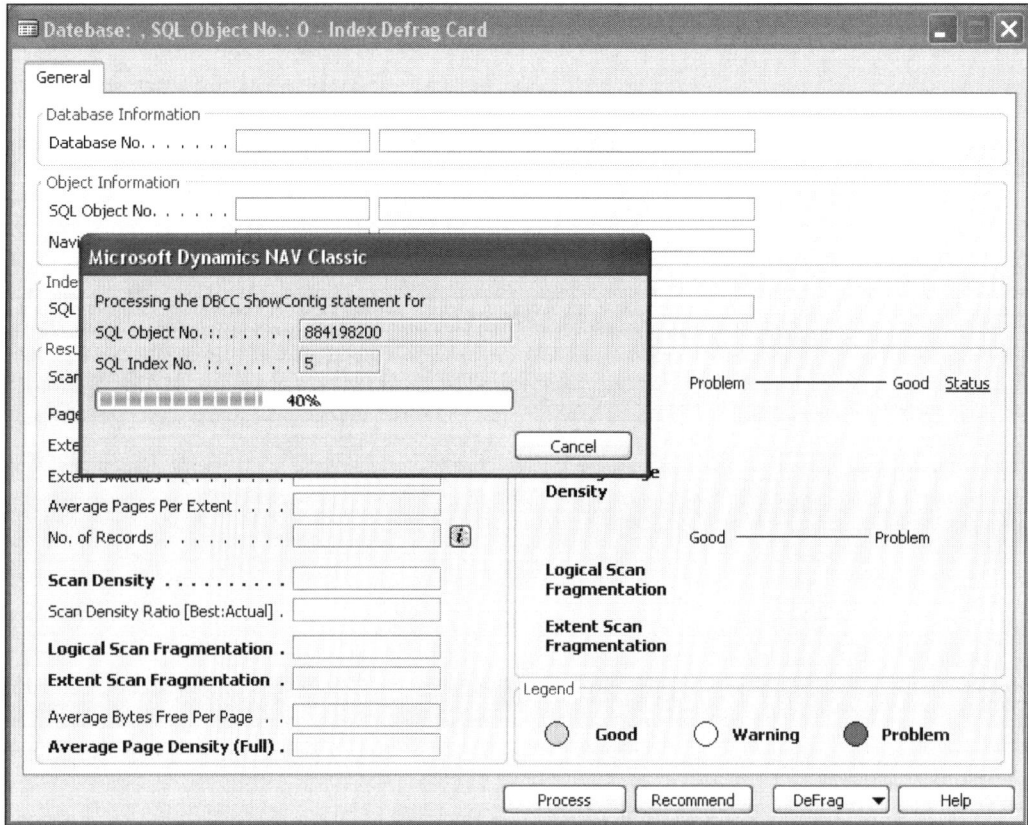

6. We can also view the recommendations made by the tool and the suggested indexes for defrag or rebuild. Click on the **Recommend** button at the bottom of the form and click **Generate** on that form to see a list of indexes. Additional check marks can be placed on the rightmost columns for **Index Defrag** and **Database ReIndex**. The ones that are check marked already are the recommendations by the tool. Use the functions listed in the **Recommend** menu button at the bottom to execute the SQL queries generated in the process.

7. The tool also creates the SQL scripts and stores them in the specified folders.

> It is worth noting that a defrag will try to reorganize the index more effectively, and the rebuild just drops the index completely and rebuilds it from scratch.

The Key Information tool

Use the `Key Information Tool.fob` to use the Key Information tool and gather additional information about various keys in the tables of the database as follows:

1. Run the form **50070, Key Information**. The initial server setup is similar to the Index Defrag tool mentioned earlier. Also, it can be accessed from the menu button **Key info | Setup SQL Connection**.

2. An additional setup needs to be done to specify what percentage of empty SIFT(s) and key fields is the threshold for the tool to change the color of the data. This can be accessed from **Key Info | Key Information Setup**. The default values are 80 percent.

3. Export the tables from the database (as a `.txt` file) and provide the path of the `.txt` file by clicking the **Load Text Objects** option at the bottom of the form.

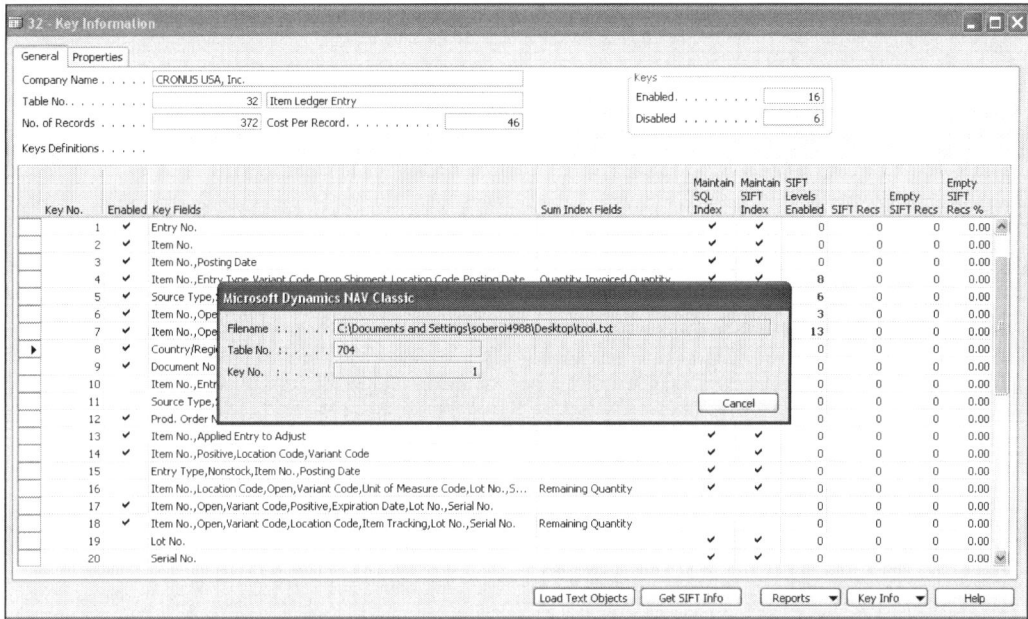

4. The tool now reads all the key information from tables and presents that in an easily navigated format.

5. To investigate a particular table, scroll left or right to the appropriate table and select a key that we want to know about. In the following example, we are looking at the **Item Ledger Entry** table and the following key: **Item No.,Open,Variant Code,Positive,Location Code,Posting Date,Expiration Date,Lot No.,Serial No. 13.** SIFT levels are enabled for this key and we can scroll down to see the SIFT levels.

32 - Key Information

General | Properties

Company Name . . . . . CRONUS USA, Inc.

Table No. . . . . 32 | Item Ledger Entry

No. of Records . . . . . 372 | Cost Per Record 46

Keys
Enabled 16
Disabled 6

Keys Definitions . . . . .

Key No.	Enabled	Key Fields	Sum Index Fields	Maintain SQL Index	Maintain SIFT Index	SIFT Levels Enabled	SIFT Recs	Empty SIFT Recs	Empty SIFT Recs %
1	✔	Entry No.		✔	✔	0	0	0	0.00
2	✔	Item No.		✔	✔	0	0	0	0.00
3	✔	Item No.,Posting Date		✔	✔	0	0	0	0.00
4	✔	Item No.,Entry Type,Variant Code,Drop Shipment,Location Code,Posting Date	Quantity,Invoiced Quantity	✔	✔	8	0	0	0.00
5	✔	Source Type,Source No.,Item No.,Variant Code,Posting Date	Quantity	✔	✔	6	0	0	0.00
6	✔	Item No.,Open,Variant Code,Positive,Location Code,Posting Date	Quantity,Remaining Quantity	✔	✔	3	0	0	0.00
7	✔	Item No.,Open,Variant Code,Positive,Location Code,Posting Date,Expirat...	Quantity,Remaining Quantity	✔	✔	13	0	0	0.00
8	✔	Country/Region Code,Entry Type,Posting Date		✔	✔	0	0	0	0.00
9		Document No.,Document Type,Document Line No.		✔	✔	0	0	0	0.00
10		Item No.,Entry Type,Variant Code,Drop Shipment,Global Dimension 1 Code,G...	Quantity,Invoiced Quantity	✔	✔	0	0	0	0.00
11		Source Type,Source No.,Global Dimension 1 Code,Global Dimension 2 Code,It...	Quantity	✔	✔	0	0	0	0.00
12	✔	Prod. Order No.,Prod. Order Line No.,Entry Type,Prod. Order Comp. Line No.	Quantity	✔		0	0	0	0.00
13	✔	Item No.,Applied Entry to Adjust		✔	✔	0	0	0	0.00
14	✔	Item No.,Positive,Location Code,Variant Code		✔	✔	0	0	0	0.00
15		Entry Type,Nonstock,Item No.,Posting Date		✔	✔	0	0	0	0.00
16	✔	Item No.,Location Code,Open,Variant Code,Unit of Measure Code,Lot No.,S...	Remaining Quantity	✔	✔	0	0	0	0.00
17		Item No.,Open,Variant Code,Positive,Expiration Date,Lot No.,Serial No.				0	0	0	0.00
18		Item No.,Open,Variant Code,Location Code,Item Tracking,Lot No.,Serial No.	Remaining Quantity			0	0	0	0.00
19		Lot No.		✔	✔	0	0	0	0.00
20		Serial No.		✔	✔	0	0	0	0.00

Load Text Objects | Get SIFT Info | Reports ▾ | Key Info ▾ | Help

7 - Key Field List

SIFT
No. of SIFT Recs for Key   0

Field No.	Name	Field Type	Blank SIFT Recs for Field	Blank SIFT Recs for Field %
2	Item No.	CODE	0	0.00
29	Open	BOOLEAN	0	0.00
5402	Variant Code	CODE	0	0.00
36	Positive	BOOLEAN	0	0.00
8	Location Code	CODE	0	0.00
3	Posting Date	DATE	0	0.00
6503	Expiration Date	DATE	0	0.00
6501	Lot No.	CODE	0	0.00
6500	Serial No.	CODE	0	0.00

Help

It is worth noting that Date and Text types in SIFT are not recommended due to the way the bucket tables are created and can cause performance issues and large bucket tables.

Session Monitor

The **Session Monitor** tool for Dynamics NAV Classic database server and for Dynamics NAV SQL database can be used to find out which sessions/users are causing the locks/blocks, to monitor I/O CPU usage, and many more.

Optimizing tables from the Dynamics NAV interface

The Dynamics NAV client for SQL Server provides an optimization tool that can be used to optimize tables.

For each table in Dynamics NAV, all SQL indexes, except the primary key, are rebuilt using the following SQL statement (this gets executed in the background when we click **Optimize**):

```
CREATE …. INDEX …. WITH DROP_EXISTING
```

To use the "optimize" feature in Dynamics NAV, follow these steps:

1. Go to **File | Database | Information**.

2. In the **Database Information** window, highlight the table(s) that we need to optimize, and click on the **Optimize** button at the bottom of the form as shown in the following screenshot:

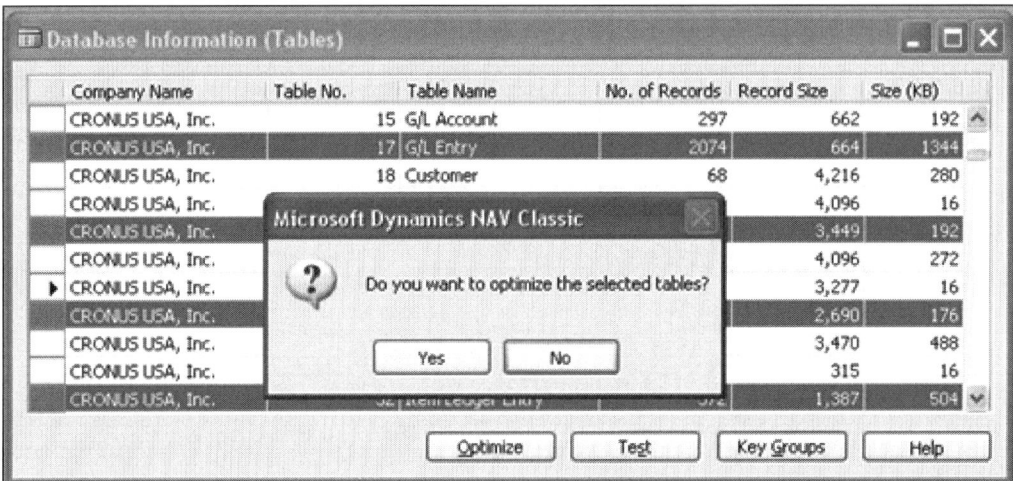

3. A progress bar takes us through the entire optimization process for the selected tables.

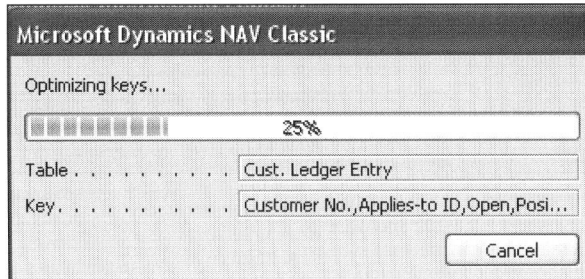

The main advantages of optimizing the tables include improved performance as a result of improved layout and defragmentation of indexes. It is also to be noted that SIFT index views are cleared of any zero values to free up additional space and improve SIFT performance.

Summary

We configured a SQL Server database for Microsoft Dynamics NAV by defining database and transaction log files, configuring RAID 10, and defining rules using collations. We also saw how we can write less expensive C/AL code with the help of the following:

*   Using FINDFIRST, FINDLAST, FINDSET, NEXT, and ISEmpty statements
*   Locking the recordset
*   Disabling the "find-as-you-type" feature

We also looked into fine-tuning the performance of the database for Dynamics NAV by using Sum Index Flow Technology, and by accessing and modifying the properties of the indexes. Finally, we looked at identifying and troubleshooting performance issues by updating the statistics and using the tools available in the SQL Resource Kit.

7
Setting up Periodic Activities, Stylesheets, and Rapid Implementation Methodology

The first part of this chapter explains periodic jobs in NAV. In the periodic jobs sections, we will learn how to set up recurring jobs, which can be run automatically at a preset time and a set frequency, for example, printing a sales report every morning or running customer reminder task every day. In NAV, all this can be done using a module called **Job Queue**.

In the latter part of this section, we will discuss the functional aspects and some of the most common batch jobs that are required in business, for example, cost adjustments, period closing, and so on.

The second part of the chapter talks about rapid implementation in NAV. The rapid implementation approach or **RIM (Rapid implementation methodology)** is a set of tools available for importing and setting up of data in a simple and easy way, using predefined templates and questionnaires.

Job Queue

Those who are familiar with prior versions of NAV might remember Job Scheduler from previous versions. Job Queue was introduced in NAV 5.0 with similar functionality to Job Scheduler, but with a changed setup and architecture. Job Scheduler required a dedicated NAV client to be run in the background, which meant an extra NAV session was always occupied. With Job Queue, we don't require a dedicated client to be always running. Job Queue runs on NAS.

Setting up Job Queue

We need to make sure the NAS is running. The setup parameter should be JOBQUEUE in NAS. Refer to *Chapter 2, Installing Dynamics NAV*, for NAS setup details.

Job Queue can be set up from both the Classic and the RoleTailored client.

In the RoleTailored client, we can find the **Job Queue** menu under **Administration | Application Setup**.

> In the **Job Queue Setup**, we need to make sure that the **Job Queue Active** option is unchecked before the setup and while changing any setup parameters. The option has to be checked after the setups are complete.

To set up a new job, under the lists, click on **Job Queue Entries** to see the list of existing entries or to create or modify entries.

Click **New** to create a new entry.

As an example, let's set up a routine to run "adjust costs" automatically everyday and we would like this batch job to run at night when the users are logged off. So every day we get updated costs of our items. **Report 795, Adjust Cost - Item Entries** is the one used to adjust item costs.

In the **Object type to Run** field, select **Report**. The options are **Report** or **CodeUnit**. Both reports and Codeunits can be used to run procedures. In NAV, reports are used not only for reporting data, but also to sometimes run repetitive procedures or loop-type programs. Therefore, depending on the need, sometimes NAV reports are preferred over Codeunits by programmers.

In the **Object ID to Run** field, look up the field to choose **795, Adjust Cost - Item Entries**. We can leave the **Parameter String** field blank for this example. This field is used to enter the text string that is used as a parameter by the job.

Let's fill the other fields as follows:

- **User ID**: This field contains the User ID of the logged in user and is filled automatically by the system.

- **Maximum No. of Attempts to Run**: Use this field to specify how many times the system should attempt running the job in the case of failure in the first attempt. Sometimes, other resources available to run the job might not be available; hence, holding up the job from starting.

- **No. of Attempts to Run**: This field contains the number of attempts that have been made to run the task. The value is incremented by one every time an attempt is made to run, till it reaches the value specified in **Maximum No. of Attempts to Run** field, after which an error is generated.

- **Last Modified Date/Time**: This shows the time stamp of when the job was last modified.

- **Expiration Date/Time**: This shows the time/date when the task should expire.

- **Earliest Start Date/Time**: This shows the time/date when the job should be run first.

- **Priority**: Use this field to set priority for the job. The higher the value, the higher is the priority of the task.

- **Status**: Describes the current status such as **Ready**, **In Process**, or **On Hold**. The default value is **On Hold**. The status needs to be changed to **Ready** by the user. The status is changed to **In Process** when the job is running.

- **Recurring Job**: This **Boolean** field is used to specify whether or not the job is a recurring one. The other days, fields under the **Recurrence** tab are used to determine whether the job should run on the specified days.

- **Starting Time**: This field is used to specify the start time of the job per run.

- **Ending Time**: This field is used to specify the latest time the job can be run. This is particularly helpful if there are multiple jobs to be run. Then the system will stop attempting to run the job after the time specified in this field, so that other jobs can be executed. This is also useful to stop the process overrunning and causing performance degradation when the users are in the system.

After all the parameters have been specified, change the status of the job to **Ready** by clicking **Reset Status**, as shown in the following screenshot:

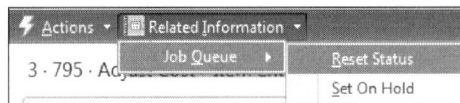

Now check the **Job Queue Active** in the **Job Queue Setup** field as shown next:

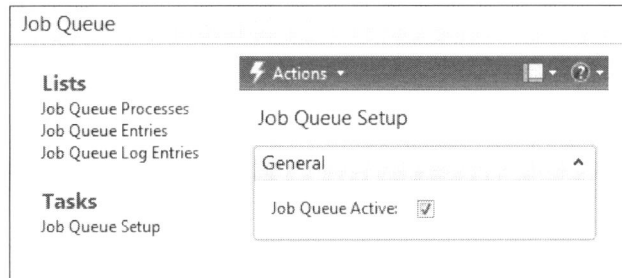

Common batch jobs

Once we know how to set up Job Queue, let's take a look at some examples of periodic jobs, which many businesses need.

Recurring journals

Recurring journals are transactions that we repeat periodically, such as monthly payments, invoices, accruals, and other repeatable entries. In NAV, a recurring journal is like a general journal with extra fields to manage reoccurrence of transactions. A recurring setup can be used for fixed amounts and/or account balances, actual or budget amounts, allocations to different balancing accounts, departments, dimensions, and many more. Let's now understand all the fields in a recurring journal.

The important fields to be filled in a recurring journal are **Recurring Method**, **Recurring Frequency**, **Posting Date**, **Document No.**, **Account Type**, **Account No.**, **Description**, and **Amount**.

The **Recurring Method** field determines how the amount on the journal line is treated in repeated transactions. For example, the **Same Amount** option uses the same value in every transaction. Hence, the amount is not deleted after the posting. These types of transactions are helpful where the amount is known every time, for example, monthly rental transactions. If the amount is unknown and needs to change every time, we can use the variable in the recurring method.

Options	Description
Fixed:	The amount on the journal is unchanged and thus will remain after posting.
Variable:	The amount on the journal is variable for the user to enter every time and, therefore, will be deleted after posting.
Balance:	The posted amount on the account on the line will be allocated among the accounts specified for the line in the general journal allocation table. The balance on the account will thus be set to zero.
	Remember to fill in the **Allocation %** field in the allocation list table.
Reversing Fixed:	The amount on the journal line will remain after posting, and a balancing entry will be posted on the next day.
Reversing Variable:	The amount on the journal line will be deleted after posting, and a balancing entry will be posted on the next day.
Reversing Balance:	The posted amount on the account on the line will be allocated among the accounts specified for the line in the general journal allocation table. The balance on the account will thus be set to zero. A balancing entry is posted on the next day.

Creating a Reminders batch job

The **Reminders batch job** is used to create reminders for customers with outstanding balances. The function uses the reminder terms code and fin charge terms code of the customer card to determine the relevant terms for the reminder. The document date triggers the use of the batch job and all ledger entries within that date, which are used when creating reminders using this function. Based on the combination of the two, the function determines if there are any additional fees or interest to be posted.

The next step is to set up the criteria for sending the first, second, and third notice to customers. In NAV this is done using levels in reminders. Level 1 is the first reminder we send regarding an overdue amount. Level 2 is the second reminder, and so on. For each reminder level, we can define a grace period and a due date. We also specify whether or not interest or an additional fee should be included on the reminder.

The following screenshot shows the **Reminder Terms** window accessed from the customer page:

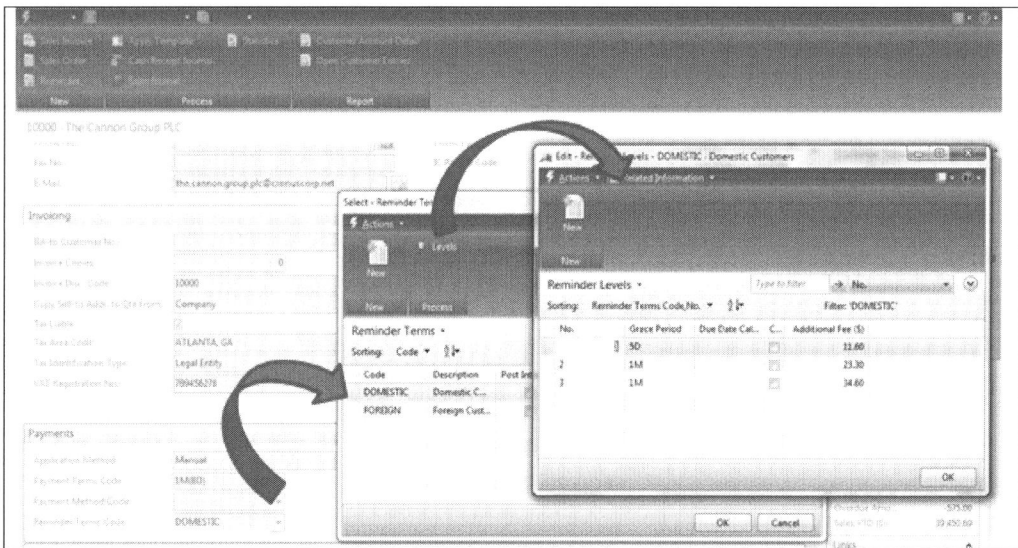

We can access the **Reminder Terms** window from **Advance | Levels | Payments | Customer Page**.

Adjust Exchange Rates batch job

The **Adjust Exchange Rates** batch job can be used to adjust G/L, customer, vendor, and bank account entries, if the exchange rate has changed as the entries were posted. The batch job doesn't replace or edit existing entries but posts additional offsetting entries to match the changes.

The system uses the **Adjustment Exchange Rate** field in the currency table to make exchange rate adjustments (gain and loss entries) to G/L, customer, vendor, and bank entries.

Let's take a look at the fields in the batch job:

- **Starting Date**: Enter a date to specify the beginning of the period for which entries will be adjusted. This can be left blank.

- **Ending Date**: Enter the last date for which entries will be adjusted. Usually, it's the same as the posting date in the **Posting Date** field.

- **Posting Description**: The user can enter any description text. The default text is **Exchange Rate Adjmt. of %1 %2** , in which **%1** is replaced by the currency code and **%2** is replaced by the currency amount that is adjusted (for example, **Exchange Rate Adjmt. of CAD,$12,600**).

- **Posting Date**: Enter the date on which the G/L entries will be posted. This date is usually the same as the ending date in the **Ending Date** field.

- **Document No.**: Enter a document number that will appear on the G/L entries created by the batch job.

- **Adjust Customer, Vendor and Bank Accounts**: Place a check mark in this field if we want to adjust customer, vendor, and bank accounts for currency fluctuations.

- **Adjust G/L Accounts for Add.-Reporting Currency**: This is required only if we use additional reporting currency and if we want to post-in an additional reporting currency. Also, if we want to adjust G/L accounts for currency fluctuations between $ and the additional reporting currency, we can make use of this feature.

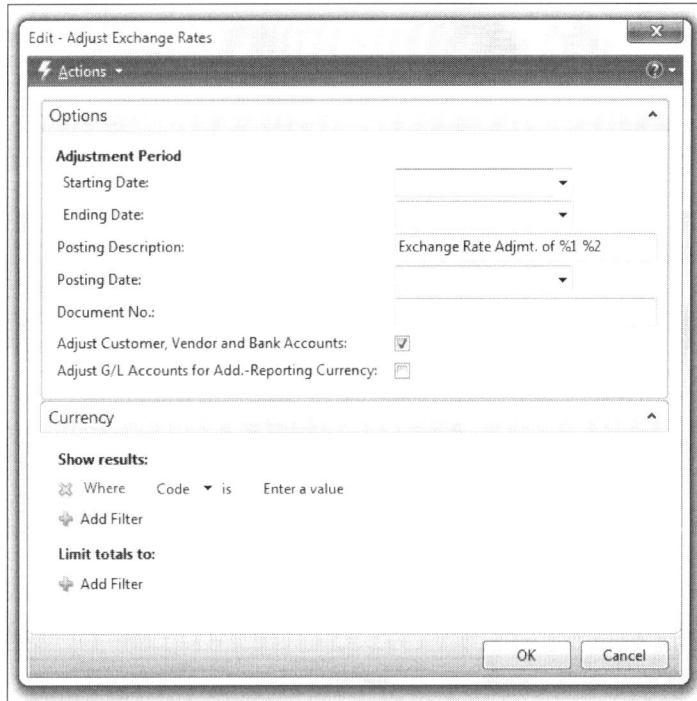

Managing stylesheets in Dynamics NAV

Sending documents to MS Word had always been a challenge in NAV, until the new "export to Excel" and "export to Word" functionality was introduced in NAV version 5 and carried over to version 2009. Automatic "Send to Excel" and "Send to Word" capability uses stylesheets to format the output from almost any page in Dynamics NAV. Just click a button, and the information will be displayed on a Word document or an Excel spreadsheet. The output is nicely formatted using the XML stylesheets, which can be structured into proper rows and columns with row headers, descriptions, field captions, logos, other pictures, and many more.

The initial version of this functionality required XML designing in order to preformat stylesheets, which required programming knowledge. However, with the new stylesheet tool, users can design new or edit existing stylesheet formats with no programming knowledge.

In this chapter, we will learn the use of the stylesheet tool to create stylesheets for Word documents:

1. To start using this tool, import the **Style Sheet Tool v2** from **Customer Source**. The ZIP file can be extracted to the FOB file. Import all objects using the object designer. The system will create 19 new objects and replace "Codeunit 403," once all the objects are imported.

   In this example, we are going to create a stylesheet format for a customer list with number, name, credit limit, and balance.

2. The stylesheet designer can be used by running **Style Sheet card(Form 680)** in the **Object Designer** using the Classic client. Create a new record for the new stylesheet.

3. Enter the relevant code and description. For example, for the **Customer List** we can use **CUST** and **Customer** fields respectively.

4. Choose the setup as shown in the previous screenshot.

5. Click **Style Sheet | Select Fields** to open the **Fields Used List** window. These fields are the ones we want to show in the final Word document.

6. In the **Field No.** field, click the **Assist** button, and in the **Style Sheet Field List** window, select the fields we want in the Word document. For example, **No.**, **Name**, **Credit Limit**, and **Balance**.

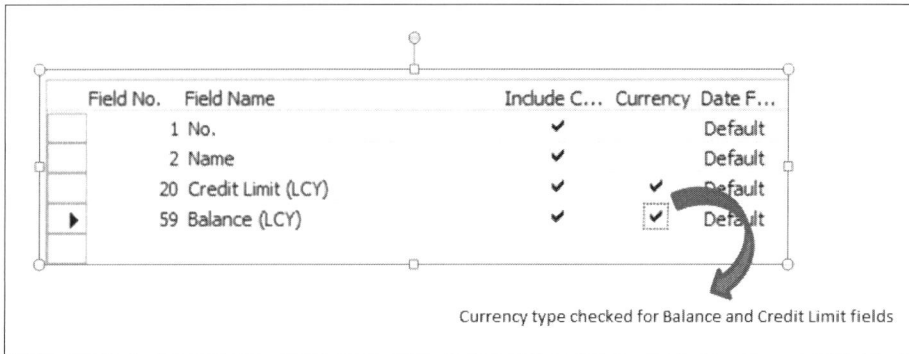

Field No.	Field Name		Include C...	Currency	Date F...
1	No.		✔		Default
2	Name		✔		Default
20	Credit Limit (LCY)		✔	✔	Default
59	Balance (LCY)		✔	✔	Default

Currency type checked for Balance and Credit Limit fields

7. The **Include Caption** checkbox in the **Item – Style Sheet Fields Used List** window has automatically been selected for each field, based on the stylesheet setup settings. This will make the caption of the fields available in our Word document. If we don't want captions but only want the data fields to be visible on our document, clear the checkbox for the field captions we don't want.

8. The **Currency** checkbox is used to display currency-related fields and are displayed with two decimals in the final Word document. In this example, we can check the **Currency Box** for the **Credit Limit** and **Balance** fields. If we don't check it, the number of decimals in the original data field, will be displayed.

9. Close the **Fields Selection** window, and the **Fields Selected** field in the **Style Sheet Card** form should be automatically checked.

10. In the **Style Sheet** menu, click on **Create Mail Merge** and this will open the Word document for us. Under the **Mailings** tab, click on **Insert Merge Field** to open the list of fields we want to insert in the Word document.

(The following screenshot shows an example of how this would look in the MS Word 2010 version, but this should be similar for Word 2007):

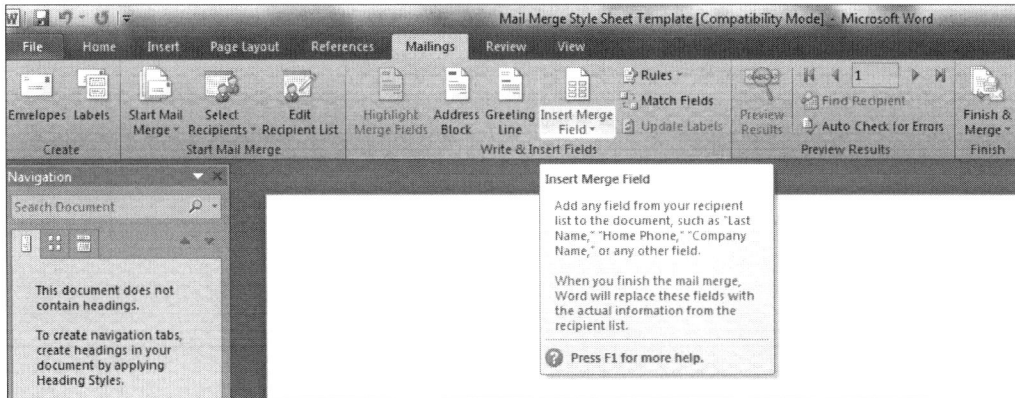

We can design the document as necessary by adding our own text and pictures.

1. The mail merge could look like the following screenshot:

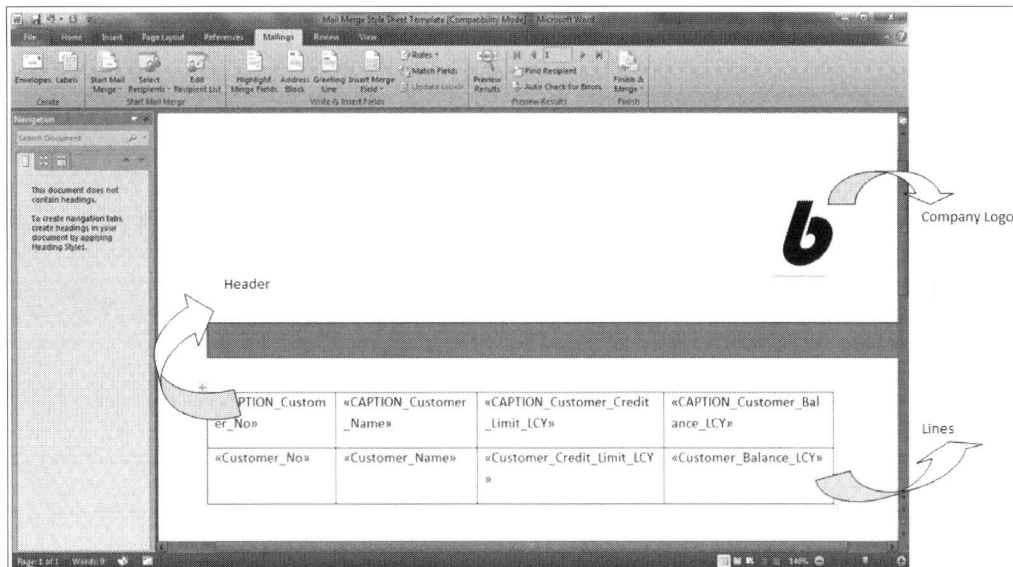

2. Close the Word document and click **Yes** to import the mail merge document. Click **Yes** to convert the mail merge document to a stylesheet document and **Yes** to update **Manage Style Sheets**. This will associate the stylesheet we just created with the customer list.

3. Now, to see the output of the stylesheet we just created, go to the **Customer List** and click on the **Word** icon. This should export the customer list in the Word document and the output should look like the following screenshot:

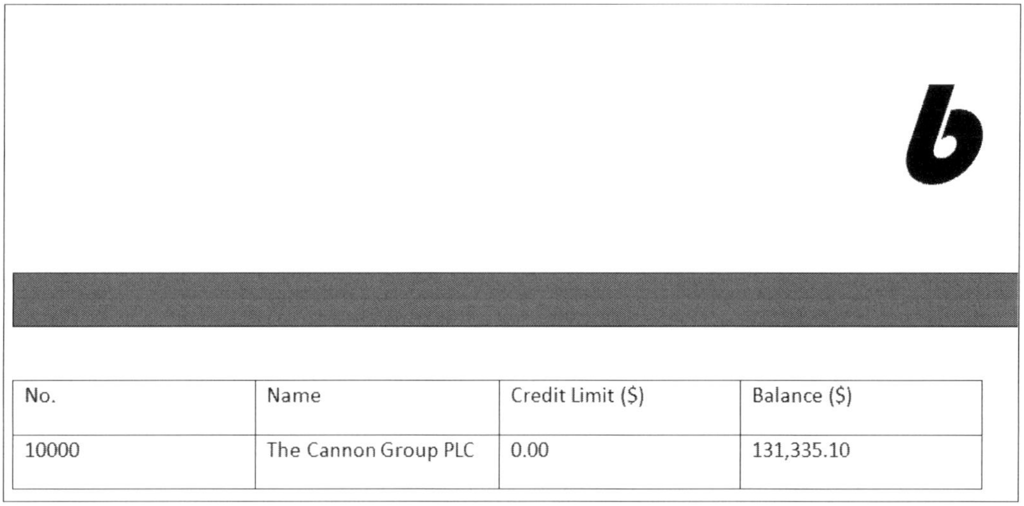

No.	Name	Credit Limit ($)	Balance ($)
10000	The Cannon Group PLC	0.00	131,335.10

The definitions of fields and menu buttons on the **Style Sheet Card** are as follows:

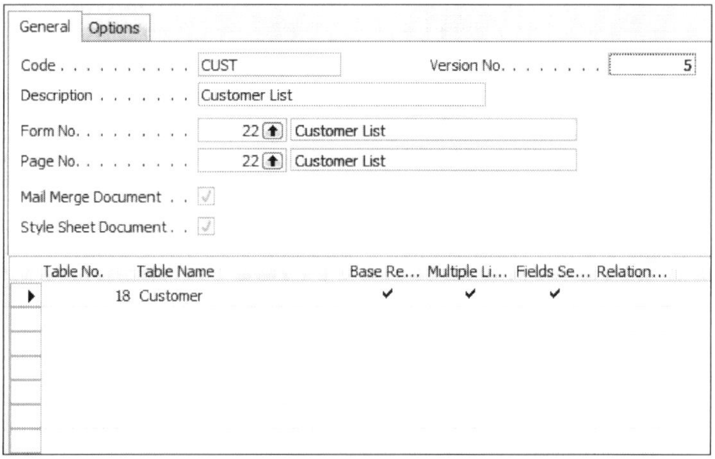

- **Code**: Used to enter alphanumeric code for this stylesheet, for example **CUST**.

- **Description**: Name or description of the stylesheet.

- **Form No.**: Lookup to select the form we want to associate with this stylesheet; this document will open when using the "export to Word" function on the customer card.

- **Page No.**: Similar to **Form No.**, pages are used in the RoleTailored client in NAV 2009 or later versions; but the functionality of exporting to Word is the same as in forms.

- **Mail Merge Document**: This field is automatically selected if there is a mail merge document associated with the stylesheet.

- **Style Sheet Document**: Similar to the **Mail Merge Document** field, this field is also automatically selected if there is a stylesheet associated to the document.

- **Version No.**: This field shows the version of the stylesheet document. The version is automatically updated every time any changes are made to the stylesheet.

- **Table No.** and **Table Name**: Shows the object number and the name of the table used.

- **Base Record**: This is the base table used in this stylesheet form. We can use as many tables in a single stylesheet without having a direct relationship with the base table, but there must be one base record on every stylesheet. This table is used to relate to the other tables that are used for setting up table relationships.

- **Multiple Lines**: This field is used if we want to have multiple lines for a record. For example, list pages or document pages with header and lines, where we have multiple lines related to a single header record.

  To use multiple lines, we will need to create a table in Word with the relevant fields and use the **MULTILINE_BEGIN_XX** tag. This tag can be found under the **Mail Merge** menu in MS Word.

> If we want a limited number of lines, we can use filters on the main page or form. The exported data follows the filters used on the main page.

- **Fields Selected**: This field is selected automatically, if we have selected one or more fields on the stylesheet.

- **Relationships**: Select this field if we have defined any relationship with the base record.

- **Select Fields**: Use this option to select the fields that we want to include in the stylesheet by table. If the **Include Captions** checkbox is selected, then the field caption for that field will be included in the stylesheet document.

- **Currency**: This checkbox is selected only for decimal type fields; then the field will be displayed with two decimals.

Note: The number of decimal places are "not" taken from the rounding precision or any other setting for the stylesheet document.

- **Assign Table Relationship**: This option allows us to define the table relationships to the base record.

Field No.	Field Name	Related-t...	Related-to Field Name	Constant Value
3	Customer No.	1	No.	
0		0		

- **Create Mail Merge**: This option allows us to create our stylesheet in MS Word. When we close Word, we will be asked if we want to import the mail merge document and if we want to convert the document to a stylesheet.

- **Open Mail Merge**: This command allows us to open the stored mail merge document. If we make changes, we can reconvert it to a stylesheet with the **Convert Mail Merge to Style Sheet** option.

- **Update Manage Style Sheets**: This command creates a record in the stylesheet table (2000000066) so that we can use the new stylesheet in the rest of the Microsoft Dynamics NAV stylesheet implementation.

The options under **Manage** menu are as follows:

- **Mail Merge Document** (**Import**, **Export**, and **Remove**): These options allow us to import, export, or remove the Word document associated with the stylesheet

- **Style Sheet Document** (**Import**, **Export**, and **Remove**). These options allow us to import, export, or remove the associated XML stylesheet object

- **Definition Import and Export**: These options allow us to export and import style definitions

After importing the document, we need to update the stylesheet using the **Update Manage Style Sheet** option.

Let's walk through the options under the **Style Sheet** setup:

General	Role Tailored Client
Show Process Dialogs . .	☑
Debug	☐
Location for XML Data File	
Include Captions Default.	☑

- **Show Process Dialogs**: This option allows the user to see the progress of all stylesheet processes. If this is not selected, then the user will see only the dialog boxes where user input is required.

- **Debug**: This option is used to debug the XML data file for any error corrections and so on.

- **Location for XML file**: This specifies the location where the debug file is stored.

- **Includes Captions Default**: By checking this option, the captions are automatically included in the mail merge document. The user can still choose not to include a particular caption by not adding it in the actual document.

Let's walk through the options under the **Role Tailored Client** tab:

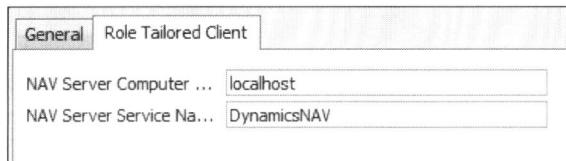

General	Role Tailored Client
NAV Server Computer ...	localhost
NAV Server Service Na...	DynamicsNAV

- **NAV Server Computer Name**: This is the name of the NAV server computer that we connect to, with the RoleTailored client.

- **NAV Server Service Name**: This is the name of the NAV server service that we connect to, with the RoleTailored client. The default value is **Dynamics NAV**.

Let's walk through the options under the **Options** tab:

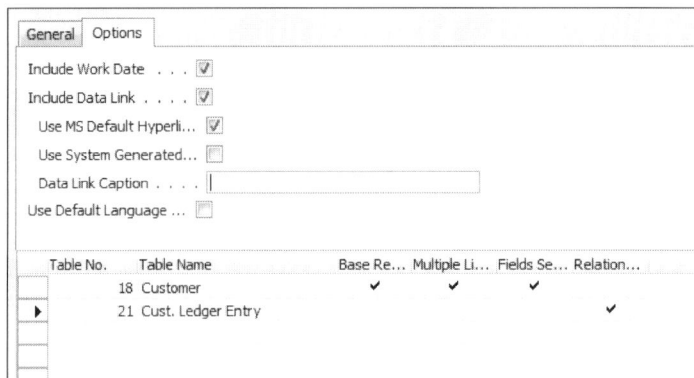

General	Options			
Include Work Date	. . .	☑		
Include Data Link	. . . .	☑		
Use MS Default Hyperli...	☑			
Use System Generated...	☐			
Data Link Caption	. . . .			
Use Default Language ...	☐			

Table No.	Table Name	Base Re...	Multiple Li...	Fields Se...	Relation...
	18 Customer	✓	✓	✓	
▶	21 Cust. Ledger Entry				✓

- **Include Work Date**: We can use this option to add a field in the mail merge document that will be replaced at runtime with the work date in the Word document.

- **Include Data Link**: This feature allows us to add a field that will be replaced at runtime with the actual link back to the original form or page, where the stylesheet was run.

Rapid Implementation Methodology

Rapid Implementation Methodology (RIM) tools were introduced in Dynamics NAV with the purpose of providing powerful tools to automate and expedite implementations. RIM tools can be used for NAV setups, data migration, importing master data, setting up industry-specific data, and other data migration requirements.

RIM tools help to bring down the total cost of ownership for customers, by providing tools for setups and data migration, which can be used by customer themselves and hence use partner resources for more specialized and value-added customization tasks.

RIM comes with various standard industry templates helpful in setting up industry-specific master data, including industry-specific questionnaires, product posting groups, customer posting groups, and many more.

Using RIM tools to set up a new company

In addition to the traditional company setup as explained in the previous chapters, RIM tools can be used to set up a new company using one of the industry-specific templates. Currently, RIM comes with the following industry templates:

- Food
- Furniture
- High Tech
- Machinery
- Wholesale

Let's take an example of setting up a new Furniture company called "Cronus Furniture Inc.":

1. From the **File** menu select **Company** | **New** as shown in the following screenshot:

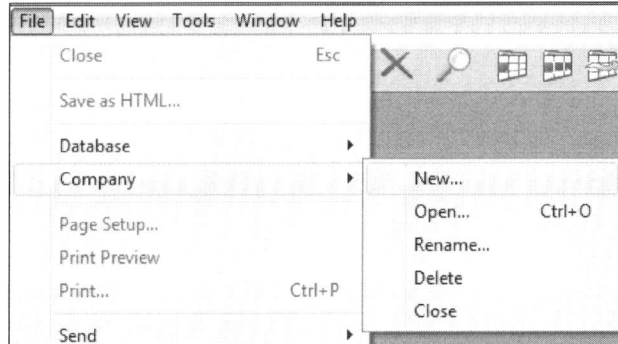

2. Fill in the name "Cronus Furniture Inc." and select **OK**.

3. Click on the **LookUp** button to see all available industry templates. Select **Furniture** from the list as shown in the following screenshot:

4. After all the data is imported and set up, the new company confirmation message will appear as shown in the next screenshot:

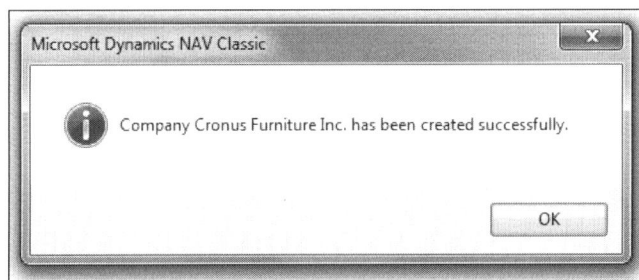

5. To check the setup data, open the newly created company. Under the **Application Setup** menu, open **Company Setup**, and then **Setup Questionnaire**.

6. On the right-side window, choose a category of questions by pressing *F5* or List from the **Question** button at the bottom-right of the screen.

7. Select the code IS (**Inventory Setup**) to see the inventory setup questions.

8. The header contains the table this questionnaire relates to, such as **Table ID**, **Table Name**, and the **Details** contains the list of all questions related to **Inventory Setup**.

   The following screenshot shows questions related to **Inventory Setup**:

	Question	Answer Option	Answer	Comment	Field Name
	1 Do you want to use the Automatic Cost Posting function?	Yes,No	Yes	Enter Yes to use the Automati...	Automatic Cost Posting
	2 Do you want to post expected costs?	Yes,No		Enter Yes to post expected co...	Expected Cost Posting to G/L
	3 How do you want the program to calculate average cost? Note If you change the average cost calculation type, all entries will be adjust...	,Item,Item & Loca...		Enter "Item" to calculate one a...	Average Cost Calc. Type
	7 Do you want to copy comments from transfer order to the transfer shipment?	Yes,No	Yes	Enter Yes to copy the commen...	Copy Comments Order to Shpt
	8 Do you want to copy comments from the transfer order to the transfer receipt?	Yes,No	Yes	Enter Yes to copy the commen...	Copy Comments Order to Rcpt
	10 Enter a date formula for the outbound warehouse handling time for your company in general.	DateFormula		Enter a date formula for inbou...	Outbound Whse. Handling Tim
	11 Enter a date formula for the inbound warehouse handling time for your company in general.	DateFormula		Enter a date formula for inbou...	Inbound Whse. Handling Time
	20 Must items have a location code in order to be posted?	Yes,No		Enter Yes to require a location...	Location Mandatory
	21 Select the number series for the Items.	Code		Before working with Inventory...	Item Nos.
	22 At which rate would you like to automatically post the Cost Adjustments to the General Ledger?	Never,Day,Week,...		In this field you can set the pr...	Automatic Cost Adjustment
	23 Select the number series for the Transfer Orders.	Code		Before working with Inventory...	Transfer Order Nos.
	24 Select the number series for the Posted Transfer Shipments.	Code		Before working with Inventory...	Posted Transfer Shpt. Nos.
	25 Select the number series for the Posted Transfer Receipts.	Code		Before working with Inventory...	Posted Transfer Rcpt. Nos.
	26 Select the number series for the Nonstock Items.	Code		Before working with Inventory...	Nonstock Item Nos.
	27 Which Item Group Dimension Code would you like to use for the product groups?	Code		This field contains the dimensi...	Item Group Dimension Code
	28 Select the number series for the Inventory Put-aways.	Code		Before working with Inventory...	Inventory Put-away Nos.
	29 Select the number series for the Inventory Picking.	Code		Before working with Inventory...	Inventory Pick Nos.
	30 Select the number series for the Posted Inventory Put-aways.	Code		Before working with Inventory...	Posted Invt. Put-away Nos.
	31 Select the number series for the Posted Inventory Picking.	Code		Before working with Inventory...	Posted Invt. Pick Nos.

9. The **Answer** column is used for answering questions and mapping the answer to the **Field Name** in the right column. The answers should follow the options in the **Answer Option** column.

10. After all the questions have been answered, press *F5* or list to go to another list and fill all questions suggested in the list.

11. To check other setup data, under the **Application Setup | Company Setup | Data Migration** to see the list of tables and migrated records, open the **Inventory Posting Group Table (table 94)** and rill into the records to see all inventory posting groups populated.

12. To import more records, we can export the template in either XML or Excel format, by clicking on the functions **Export to XML** or **Export to Excel**. Select table 94 and click on the **Export to Excel** function to export the template in Excel form, as shown in the following screenshot:

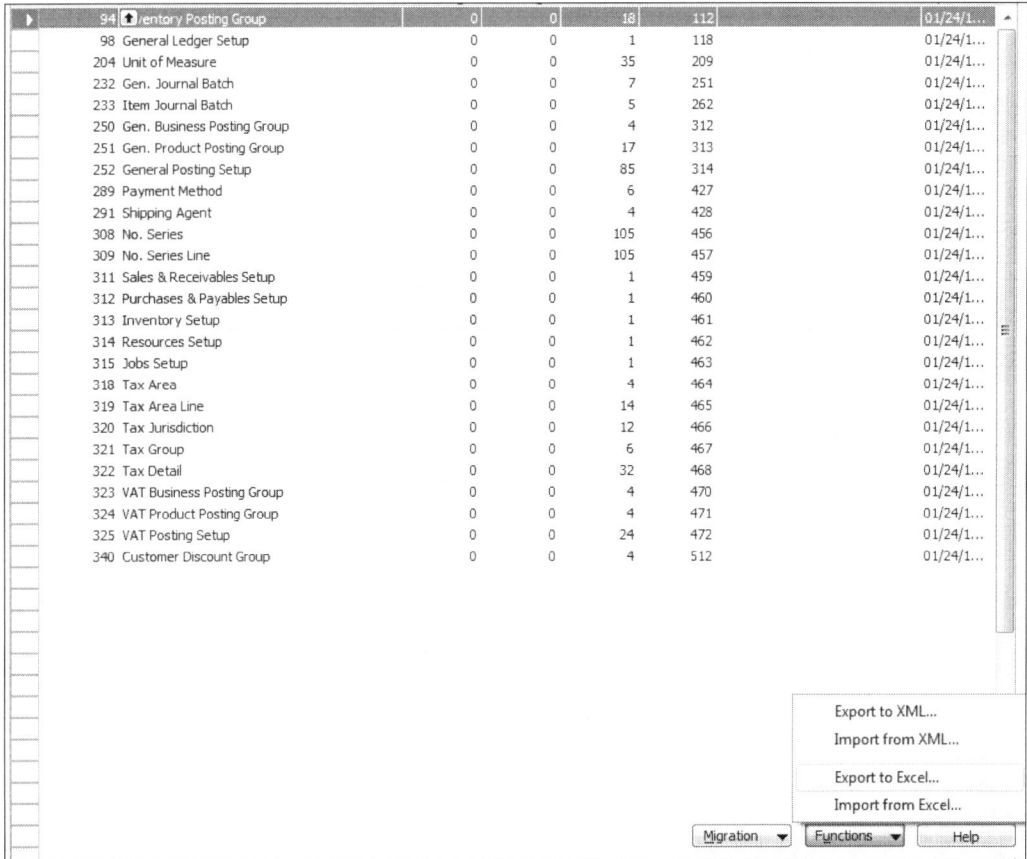

94	Inventory Posting Group	0	0	18	112		01/24/1...
98	General Ledger Setup	0	0	1	118		01/24/1...
204	Unit of Measure	0	0	35	209		01/24/1...
232	Gen. Journal Batch	0	0	7	251		01/24/1...
233	Item Journal Batch	0	0	5	262		01/24/1...
250	Gen. Business Posting Group	0	0	4	312		01/24/1...
251	Gen. Product Posting Group	0	0	17	313		01/24/1...
252	General Posting Setup	0	0	85	314		01/24/1...
289	Payment Method	0	0	6	427		01/24/1...
291	Shipping Agent	0	0	4	428		01/24/1...
308	No. Series	0	0	105	456		01/24/1...
309	No. Series Line	0	0	105	457		01/24/1...
311	Sales & Receivables Setup	0	0	1	459		01/24/1...
312	Purchases & Payables Setup	0	0	1	460		01/24/1...
313	Inventory Setup	0	0	1	461		01/24/1...
314	Resources Setup	0	0	1	462		01/24/1...
315	Jobs Setup	0	0	1	463		01/24/1...
318	Tax Area	0	0	4	464		01/24/1...
319	Tax Area Line	0	0	14	465		01/24/1...
320	Tax Jurisdiction	0	0	12	466		01/24/1...
321	Tax Group	0	0	6	467		01/24/1...
322	Tax Detail	0	0	32	468		01/24/1...
323	VAT Business Posting Group	0	0	4	470		01/24/1...
324	VAT Product Posting Group	0	0	4	471		01/24/1...
325	VAT Posting Setup	0	0	24	472		01/24/1...
340	Customer Discount Group	0	0	4	512		01/24/1...

Export to XML...

Import from XML...

Export to Excel...

Import from Excel...

Migration ▼   Functions ▼   Help

13. Select the path to save the Excel file. Open the Excel file to see the exported records. Add a new record at the end of the list as shown next and save the file.

16	OPER	Operation part
17	PACKING	Packing material
18	PARTS	Component
19	SHELVES	Shelve
20	TOP	Table
21	WARDROBE	Wardrobe
22	Test	Test Import

14. Now go back to NAV, on the same **Data Migration** screen, select table 94 and click on **Migration Records** from the **Migration** menu. The newly added record **Test** will be at the end of records. Click on **Apply** to commit the record to the table.

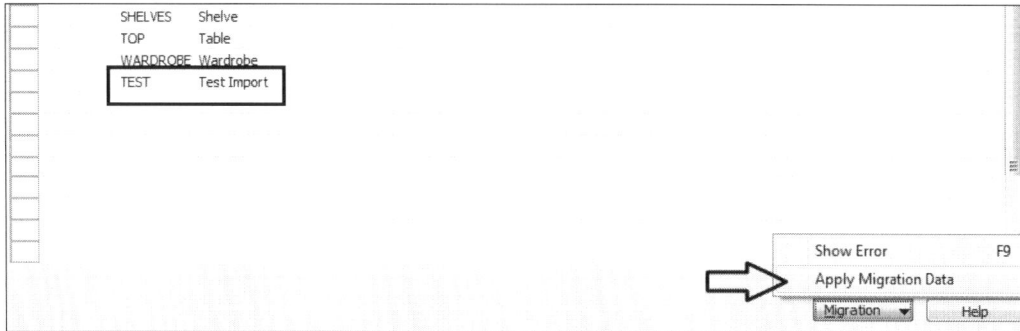

In addition to setups, the RIM data migration tool can be used for other migration records or to create our own templates. The easy Excel or XML interface can be used to add new records in predefined templates.

Summary

We started with setting up a batch job to adjust costs every day, which runs automatically at night when the users are logged off. Then we looked at some examples of periodic jobs, which included Recurring Journals, Reminders, and Adjust Exchange Rates. We then created stylesheets for Word documents using the stylesheet tool. Finally, we created our own company template using the RIM data migration tool and migrated records into it.

8
Updating Objects and Virtualization with Dynamics NAV

Dynamics NAV has long been known as a system with rich out-of-the-box capabilities and high flexibility. Although it offers a rich inherent feature set, it is also one of the most flexible systems available in the market today. Flexibility can be attained by modifying an existing set of objects or adding new objects in NAV. Objects in NAV comprise tables, reports, code units, forms, pages, and dataports and XML ports. This chapter speaks about the procedures for changing and updating these objects.

The second part of the chapter discusses some common batch jobs, their setups and procedures.

Objects in NAV

Each development element in NAV is referred to as an object. There are seven types of objects in NAV.

- Forms (used only in the Classic client)
- Pages
- Tables
- Code units
- Data ports
- XML ports
- Reports

The user can modify any of these objects provided the license has proper development privileges and object ranges. Based on the business requirements, these objects can be exported, modified, and updated in the system using the import function. The prior versions of NAV did not allow import of objects if the modified range was not included in the user's license. But starting from version 5.1, this restriction is no longer applicable. This implies that the modifications, although not in the license range, can be imported in NAV, the usage of which is still restricted by license ranges.

Updating objects

Updating objects in NAV is quite simple. However, as there is no formal object version management tool or check-in/check-out tool available in NAV, one has to be careful while updating these objects. The changes can be overwritten if two developers work on the same set of objects and update them in NAV at different times. The last update is the one that will overwrite all the preceding updates.

Though some developers have created their own versions of check-in/check-out tools using the NAV development environment, one of the most common ways is to maintain a log that shows the objects that are being used and by which developers. A development team leader or project manager can be the in charge of maintaining this list of objects.

The procedure for updating different objects is very much similar in NAV with the exception of updating tables, where merge and overwrite options are available.

Exporting the objects from NAV

Let's start with exporting the objects from NAV.

The objects can be exported in binary, `.fob`, or `.txt` structures. Multiple objects can be selected and can be exported as a single `.fob` or `.txt` file and so the naming is crucial while exporting objects. Most developers follow certain naming conventions, the most common practice being to assign a name similar to the requirements or gap ID in the Gap/Fit sheet or the functional requirements document. This way, the users can easily identify what changes the fob or txt file pertains to. Also, it is a good practice to use a short date as suffix in the export name.

For example, the following can be used to name object export files:

```
"GAP1-1A01-0210.fob"
"DescriptionFieldLengthIncrease-0210.fob"
"GAP-1A01-ver1-0.fob" etc.
```

Open the object designer of the master DB in the Classic client in NAV. The object designer is not available through the RoleTailored client as of NAV 2009 SP1. The master DB is the one that maintains the final version of all objects modified by different developers. Each developer can have their own versions of development DBs, but eventually all modified objects are updated in the master DB according to the development log.

1. Select the objects to be modified. We can then modify the objects as per the specifications document. Filters can be used to select different types of objects. It's better to keep all objects in a single `.fob` or `.txt` file.

2. The following screenshot describes the selection and export of various objects:

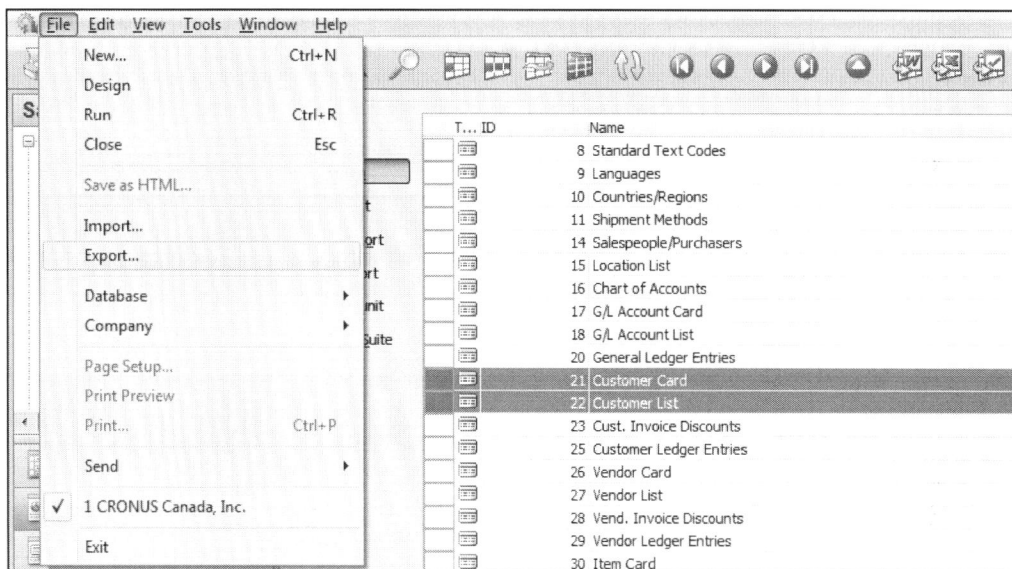

Once the objects are exported, they can be modified by the developers using their development license. The Project Manager/Development Manager at this point needs to keep a tight control on what objects are checked out by which developers. Some programmers have developed object management tools that help in monitoring the check-out and check-in of objects. If multiple developers work on the same objects, make sure that the changes are merged with the latest version of the import. The next step is to import objects.

Importing a file with modifications

Importing the objects is similar for all objects, with the exception of tables, where a merge option is available in addition to the overwrite and replace option.

Let's take an example of importing a file that has modifications related to a form and a table:

1. Open the object designer and click on **Import...**. Point to the `.fob` file with changed objects. An error message cautioning conflict of objects will appear; click on **OK**.

2. Once we click on **OK**, the system shows the import worksheet with all the objects listed. The conflicts come with a warning sign.

3. If the object ID doesn't have a conflict in import, the system imports the new objects without warning. However, if the object ID already exists in the system, it gives a warning (shown in the screenshot prior to the preceding one) and opens an import worksheet. The worksheet gives the option to handle each object in a separate line. The fields for each line and object describe details of each object and how it should be handled:

   ° **Type**: The type of the object is one of the eight object types, such as table, form, and so on.

   ° **No.**: The ID of the imported object. The ID identifies the range the object falls under. For example, a custom object using a standard developer license can fall in the 50,000 to 99,999 range. The customer is usually assigned a range in his/her license and is allowed to use customizations only in that range.

   ° **Name**: This field describes the name or description of the object. The name or description should be unique for each object in the system.

   ° **New Object**: This option is automatically checked if this is a new object.

   ° **New Object Changed**: This option is automatically checked if the new object has been marked as changed.

   ° **Action**: This is the field that the user can input to choose how to handle conflicting objects. The options are create, replace, delete, skip, merge (New <- Existing) and merge (Existing <- New). The two merge options are available only in the case of tables.

     • **Create**: The system creates a new object in the database.

     • **Replace**: The existing object will be replaced by the new version of the object.

     • **Delete**: The existing object will be deleted.

     • **Skip**: This system will skip the import of the object.

     • **Merge (Existing<-New)**: All fields in the existing table will remain and any additional fields from the new object will be added.

- **Merge** (**New<-Existing**): All fields in the new table will be imported and any additional fields in the existing table will be added to the new table.

4. Another option available is to use the **Replace All** function that replaces all objects with the new version of objects. This is a commonly used option if the user doesn't want to go through each line and manually change the option for each object. The following screenshot shows the **Replace All** function to replace all objects:

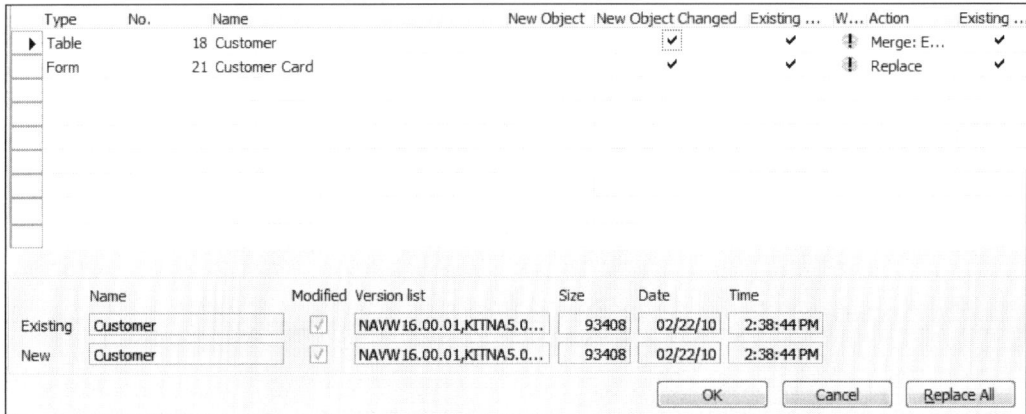

	Type	No.	Name	New Object	New Object Changed	Existing ...	W...	Action	Existing ...
▶	Table	18	Customer		✔	✔	⚠	Merge: E...	✔
	Form	21	Customer Card		✔	✔	⚠	Replace	✔

	Name	Modified	Version list	Size	Date	Time
Existing	Customer	☑	NAVW 16.00.01,KITNA5.0...	93408	02/22/10	2:38:44 PM
New	Customer	☑	NAVW 16.00.01,KITNA5.0...	93408	02/22/10	2:38:44 PM

[OK] [Cancel] [Replace All]

5. Once the objects are imported, the system displays a message box with details of how many objects were imported, created, replaced, and so on.

6. The user is now ready to use the system with the changed objects. The following screenshot shows the message box with details:

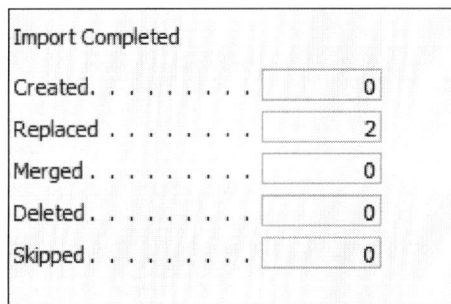

Import Completed

Created. 0

Replaced 2

Merged 0

Deleted. 0

Skipped 0

The second part of this chapter focuses on virtualization with Dynamics NAV.

Virtualization with Dynamics NAV

Virtualization has become one of the most critical aspects of IT systems today. In fact, it is one of the most talked-about buzz words in IT. However, let's first understand what exactly virtualization is, why businesses need it, and how NAV works in virtualization environments.

In simple terms, **virtualization** means to create a virtual version of a physical resource. The resource could be a physical device such as a physical server, storage device, network or programs, or even operating systems. A simple example could be that of partitioning a hard drive—we take one physical drive and partition it to create two separate hard drives.

Although there can be many detailed categorizations and sub-categorizations of virtualization, it can be broadly classified into five main categories:

- **Server virtualization**: Consolidating multiple physical servers into virtual servers that run on a single physical server.

- **Application virtualization**: An application runs on another host from where it is installed in a variety of ways.

- **Desktop virtualization**: Essentially it's the concept of separating a personal computer desktop environment from the physical machine through a remote server connection. The virtualized desktop is stored on a remote central server and so, when users work from their remote desktop client, all of the programs, applications, processes, and data used are kept and run centrally, allowing users to access their desktops on any light device that need not be as resource rich as the applications would have otherwise required.

- **Network virtualization**: With network virtualization, a physical network is logically segmented by multiplexing shared access to a single network. Resource components of a virtual network could include switches, VLANs, network storage devices, virtual network containers, and so on.

- **Storage virtualization**: This is the technique of virtualizing the disk/data storage for our data, which is consolidated to and managed by a virtual storage system.

Advantages of virtualization

The following are the advantages of virtualization:

- Virtualization results in huge savings on hardware, environmental costs, management, and administration of the server infrastructure by consolidating the workloads of several underutilized servers to fewer machines, perhaps a single machine (server consolidation).

- Virtualization is an important concept in building secure platforms by providing secure, isolated playground systems for running untrusted applications.

- Virtual machines can be used to run multiple operating systems simultaneously, different versions, or entirely different systems.

- Virtual machines can provide abstracts of hardware, or hardware configuration that we do not actually have (such as multiple CPUs, SCSI devices, and so on).

- Virtualization can make tasks such as system migration, backup, and recovery easier and more manageable.

- Apart from various other advantages, high availability is one of the many important advantages of a virtualized environment. Let's take an example of high availability with Hyper-V available using new features in Server 2008. Availability means that users can access a system to do their work. With high availability, there is a significant expectation that users will always be able to access the system, as it has been designed and implemented to ensure operational continuity. High availability for Hyper-V is achieved through the use of the Windows Server 2008 Failover Cluster feature. High availability is impacted by both planned and unplanned downtime, and failover clustering can significantly increase availability of virtual machines in both of these categories.

Virtual machines can be managed by the Failover Cluster, and the Failover Cluster can be used inside of virtual machines to monitor and move the workloads that are hosted in the virtual machine. In order to understand availability, let's take broad categories in planned and unplanned downtime scenarios:

  ○ **Guest availability**: Guests that are running Windows Server 2008 can use the Windows Failover Cluster feature to provide high availability for their workloads. There are several advantages to using Windows failover clustering inside of a guest.

  ○ **Virtual machine maintenance:** If the configuration of the VM needs to be changed or if the OS or software needs to be updated or changed, the workload can be moved to another node of the cluster and the virtual machine can either be shut down or updated with minimal interruption to the end users.

  ○ **Host machine maintenance**: If the physical machine hosting a Hyper-V VM needs maintenance or software updates and other members of the Windows Failover Cluster are located on different Hyper-V hosts, the workload on the VM can be moved to another node of the cluster and VM can be shut down to accommodate the changes or reboots of the physical server.

° **Virtual or Host Machine Failure**: If there is a failure of the physical Hyper-V host or the virtual machine guest, the other nodes of the Windows Failover Cluster will detect that the cluster member is no longer responding or participating in the cluster and the surviving nodes will bring online the applications or services that had been running on the failed VM.

Dynamics NAV and application virtualization

Dynamics NAV is widely used today in development environments with various virtualization technologies. Although there's no formal recommendation from Microsoft on the use of virtualization with NAV in production environments, various case studies and tests suggest the use of Dynamics NAV in a virtualized environment with a slight variance in performance. To study in detail how NAV is supported in virtualization environments, let's first look at the compatibility guidance on NAV with various virtualization technologies. The guidance is available on the server catalog website often suggested by the Microsoft support team for versions compatibility. Although the website details compatibility with many technologies, we will focus on the most common ones for the scope of this book. http://www.windowsservercatalog.com/

The following table shows which virtualization technologies are supported with the listed guest OS architectures:

Virtualization technology	Windows Server 2003 SP2	Windows Server 2008	Windows Server 2008 R2
Hyper V	Yes	Yes	Yes
VMWare ESX 3.5 Update 2,3,4	Yes	Yes	No
VMWare ESX 3.5 Update 3,4	Yes	Yes	Yes
VM vSphere 4	Yes	Yes	No

According to the website, *VMWare ESX 3.5 update 5* and *VM vSphere 4.0 update 1* are not supported as of now.

Guest OS x86(32 Bit) is only supported and x64 is not supported as of now.

But this compatibility guidance website or other sources should be checked for the latest and current compatibility updates.

After having gone through the compatibility guide, let's now review some performance results with NAV on some common processes.

The tests were done on Dynamics NAV 2009 SP1 on Server 2008 as host OS with HyperV. Although the tests are done using Hyper-V only, various sources suggest similar results (testing recommended) using other Hypervisor-based virtualizations such as VMWare, among others.

The scenario used three service tiers with and without HyperV on standard hardware with 75 simulated concurrent users. The tests were done using standard hardware, not high performance machines.

Similar tests scenarios can also be studied in the official hardware and performance guide provided by Microsoft for NAV 2009.

The performance difference was huge in some specific processes, but the average performance declined from anywhere between 8 percent to 40 precent in most processes. The average response time ranged from 300ms to 1100ms without Hyper-V to 330ms to 1500ms with Hyper-V. The processes for which the performance was very different were short processes ranging from 1ms to 20ms.

Although the percentagewise performance was down to an average of 8% to 40%, the actual response time differential was in the range of 30ms to 500ms depending on the process.

This might not be a big deterrent in most businesses but Microsoft Dynamics NAV should not be run in a virtualized environment purely for performance reasons; instead, other factors such as saving on hardware costs, among others, should be strongly considered for a virtualized environment.

Also, other factors such as SQL optimization should be considered. For example, adding two or more cores to the computer running Microsoft Dynamics NAV Server (according to the performance guide) gives a 5 percent gain over two cores.

Server virtualization is supported with NAV 2009 even today. But NAV 2009 R2 and future versions interfaces would allow deployment using Microsoft Application Virtualization (App-V) technology, which is relevant for both on-premise and hosted solutions.

Summary

We exported objects from NAV and imported a file that has the modifications. We looked at the different fields in the import worksheet. We then looked at what virtualization is, its types, and advantages. We then saw how Dynamics NAV is supported in virtualization. In the following chapter, we will see how we can aggregate and deliver concise information to the relevant people from different systems in a consolidated, reliable, and accurate way by using business intelligence.

9
Business Intelligence

In this chapter we will cover perhaps the most important aspect of an ERP solution—**Business Intelligence (BI)**.

Business Intelligence can be thought of as a broad category of applications, tools, technologies, and methods used to help companies get a clear view of internal and external aspects of their business to enable better decision making.

It can be defined as a set of tools that can capture, calibrate, and store information from different systems for analysis and graphic presentation of data in the form of charts, reports, key performance indicators, and dashboards.

Business Intelligence systems aim at aggregating and delivering concise information to the relevant individuals from different systems, in a consolidated, reliable, and accurate way. The same data could mean different things to different people. So, how data is presented depends on its relevance to different individuals. Let's consider an example of a customer and item ledger. The item and customer ledgers will have details of every transaction related to the customer and every entry of item movement, which might be helpful in audits; however, how does this large set of data help the CEO? The CEO needs concise information aggregated from both ledgers and presented in a "profit by categories" dashboard, or perhaps a key performance indicator that compares current sales to forecast with achieved, underperformed, or exceeded indicators. BI systems can help consolidate this data from disparate systems and represent in a relevant way to different people.

The following figure illustrates different data sources feeding information to the data warehouse and retrieving it in the form of reports, charts, graphs, and indicators:

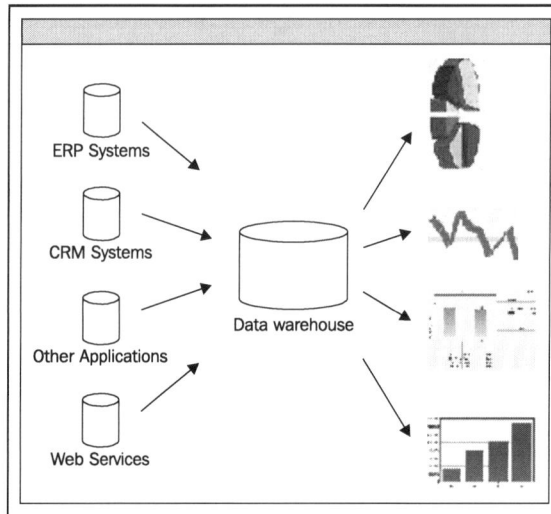

Importance of Business Intelligence

With enormous volumes of data everywhere in the systems, it's absolutely imperative to access relevant business data in order to make informed decisions. Business Intelligence is absolutely critical in helping organizations of all sizes to meet their short and long-term strategic goals.

The Microsoft Business Intelligence story

Microsoft has several Business Intelligence tools and applications with BI features, each of which is important to understand as we decide what will work best for the situation we have at hand. The BI tools we use depend on the specific problems we are trying to solve. Our daily business activities have associated information and insights that emerge in three main areas of Business Intelligence—personal, team, and organizational. There will be overlap across these areas—for example, a company's employees may use Office Excel and Excel Services in Office SharePoint Server to make relevant business decisions at the corporate level. PerformancePoint Server uses Excel, Office SharePoint Server, and Excel Services to complement its BI tools in order to deliver a corporate BI solution that has elements of personal and team BI. By design, all Microsoft BI products interoperate so that teams and individuals within an organization can move across the continuum of personnel and teams, and have all products work together.

Business Intelligence categories overview

The following table gives an overview of the three categories of Business Intelligence—Personal BI, Team BI, and Corporate BI:

Parameters	Personal BI	Team BI	Corporate BI
Usage	Personal BI delivers information to people when they need it and in the desired format. Personal BI is probably independent of a connected data store or direct involvement from the IT department.	People don't work just as individuals, but in groups and teams to complete projects. Team BI delivers information that reflects this, providing BI that focuses on accountability to promote collaboration, and rapid sharing of information to drive to a common decision.	Corporate BI describes a set of tools that help people align their objectives and activities with overall company goals, objectives, and metrics. It is BI that helps synchronize individual efforts by using scorecards, strategy maps, and other tools that connect to corporate data.
Tools used	Excel	Office SharePoint Server and Excel Services.	PerformancePoint Server 2007.
Technology built on	Can be linked to an SQL Server Analysis Services cube	Built on trusted data using Microsoft SQL Server.	Built on trusted data using Microsoft SQL Server.

Business Intelligence product scenarios

The following are brief scenarios designed to illustrate how each tool can be used in different circumstances:

Scenario and BI context	Excel	Excel Services	PerformancePoint Server
Personal BI			
End users perform quick analysis in Excel on available information.	X		
End users analyze and perform exploratory and free-form analysis on data from a variety of sources in a way that requires minimal IT involvement.	X		
End users create a quick spreadsheet-based report.	X		

Scenario and BI context	Excel	Excel Services	PerformancePoint Server
Team BI			
Microsoft Office users are enabled to easily store and share documents in a way that enhances collaboration and empowers teams to easily work together on projects and objectives.		X	
End users share their analysis in dashboards or reports with others.		X	
End users can create simple data indicator objects on a SharePoint page. The objects can query basic data sources for a value, compare the value to another value, and show the relationship with a set of standard visual indicators.		X	
End users need to secure access to the files produced.		X	
Organizational BI			
There is a need for organizational planning, budgeting, forecasting, and financial consolidation capabilities.			X
The IT department provides defined data views across the organization with business user role-defined views of metrics and strategies.			X
The IT department needs oversight into organization-wide corporate governance and compliance initiatives.			X
The IT department needs to implement an organization-wide Balanced Scorecard initiative.			X
Business users can create a "guided analytics" experience with structured data. End-users use a single application to follow a train of thought against a prebuilt data source specific to running some area of the business. End users can create dashboards that contain scorecards, KPIs, analytical reports, and analytical views against the data source and keep it in one location.			X
End users need access to unstructured data, providing context to the scorecard metric.			X
Financial business users can create consolidated financial reports without having to prebuild a financial data mart using PerformancePoint Server Management Reporter.			

Dynamics NAV and Business Intelligence

Many small to mid-sized companies usually struggle to take advantage of the right Business Intelligence due to lack of resources, proper tools, and systems that are often too expensive and complicated to deploy and maintain. With powerful inherent BI capabilities, robust cross-product integration, and advanced technology improvements Dynamics NAV 2009 provides a single-point and comprehensive business management solution with broad Business Intelligence options, which are easy to deploy, flexible to personalize and customize, and easy to maintain.

Inherent BI capabilities in NAV

Inherent BI capabilities in NAV include standard reports that take advantage of strong SQL reporting services, flexible views of data that allow various options for filtering, flexible search, flexible data view options for different people, and easy-to-use ad hoc reporting tools and charts. Record links tie together structured and unstructured information, and transactional insight can help people find documents related to specific transactions—for example, a scanned copy of a customer PO can be attached as a link to the sales order. Built-in features such as drilldowns, lookups, and flow fields among others allow real-time data in pages and provide options to navigate into details of transactions, customer and supplier records, histories, and more. The use of dimensions allows us to define and assign characteristics to the information in our daily work such as product groups, market segments, geographic regions, and time period. We can define hierarchies that reflect reporting, analysis, and accounting needs.

Business insight through the Role Center

The Role Center serves as a pivotal area for our role and provides an important insight to our business through various parts personalized according to our function in the company.

Activities section

The Activities section consists of Cues and Action items specific to the user's profile. The Cues provide a pictorial representation of an activity or task such as the number of sales orders, and the Actions provide links to triggers for particular actions such as creating orders or quotes.

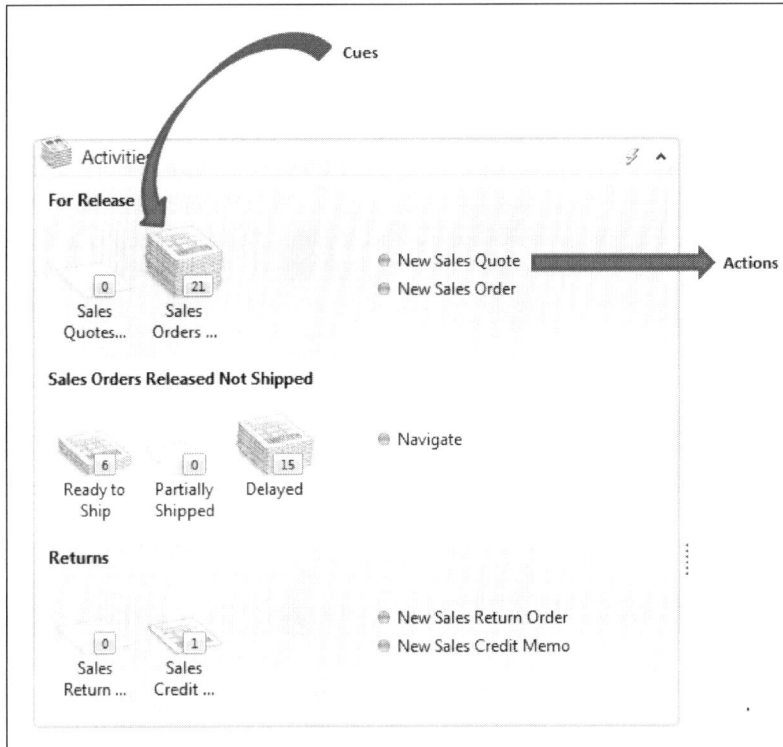

My Customers/Items/Vendors

The **My Customers** section provides quick links to our top customer pages and high-level details such as **Customer No.**, **Phone No.**, and so on. This applies to the **My Vendors** and **My Items** sections as well.

My Notifications

The **My Notifications** section provides a space for instant notifications between peers and colleagues. We can also attach links to actual items and other entities in our communication.

> With the ability to add external objects in the NAV RoleTailored client, the users can create visual objects, KPIs, graphs, and other Business Intelligence objects and add them in different sections of pages. This capability is described in detail in *Chapter 3, Integrating Dynamics NAV to Microsoft Platform*.

Graphical charts and ad hoc analysis

NAV 2009 introduced a feature to create ad hoc charts in list pages. The user can create a two-or three-dimensional chart in any page, which displays the data relevant for the user in a graphical representation.

Let's see an example of creating a chart to analyze the status of inventory in terms of demand and supply:

1. From the Role Center, open the Items page. The page lists all the items in the system. To make the data relevant, let's apply some filters on this list. We can use the expand option to see the full list of filters.

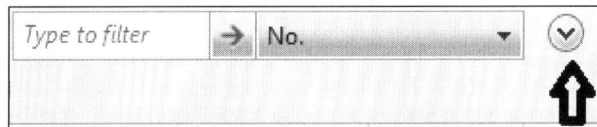

2. Select the **No.** range using the **No.** filter. We can use the **Add Filter** function if we need to add multiple filters to view the data.

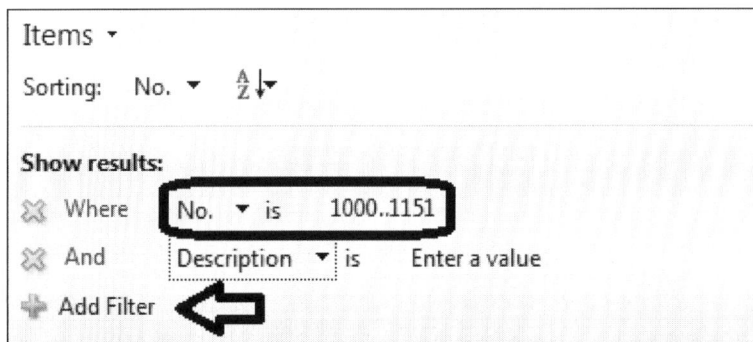

No.	Description	Sub...	Productio...	Routing No.	Base Unit ...	C...	Unit Cost	Unit Price	Vendor No.
1000	Bicycle	No	1000	1000	PCS		350.595	4,000.00	
1001	Touring Bicycle	No	1000	1000	PCS	☑	350.595	4,000.00	
1100	Front Wheel	No	1100	1100	PCS		129.671	1,000.00	20000
1110	Rim	No			PCS	☑	1.05	0.00	01587796
1120	Spokes	No			PCS	☑	2.00	0.00	01587796
1150	Front Hub	No	1150	1150	PCS	☑	12.441	500.00	
1151	Axle Front Wheel	No			PCS	☑	0.45	0.00	32456123

3. From the **Customize page** option on the top-right corner, select the **Chart Pane** option.

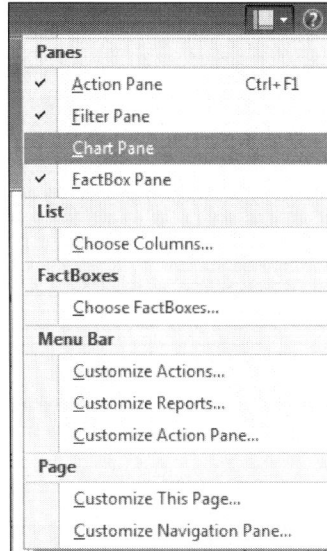

4. This should bring up a blank chart at the bottom. The first step is to select **Measures** from the top-left corner of the chart. You can select as many measures as you want at the same time. For this example, we will select three measures: **Qty. on Sales Orders**, **Qty. on Purchase Orders**, and **Qty. on Hand**.

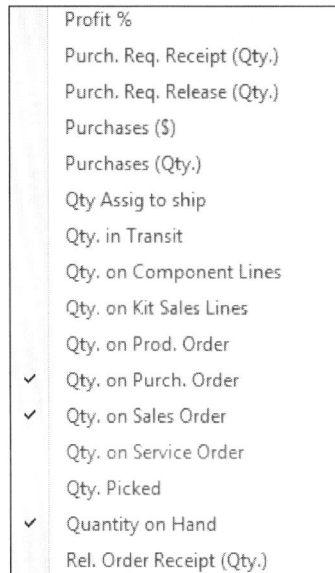

5. Select the **Description** dimension from the bottom-right corner of the chart. Once selected, the analysis should be like the following screenshot:

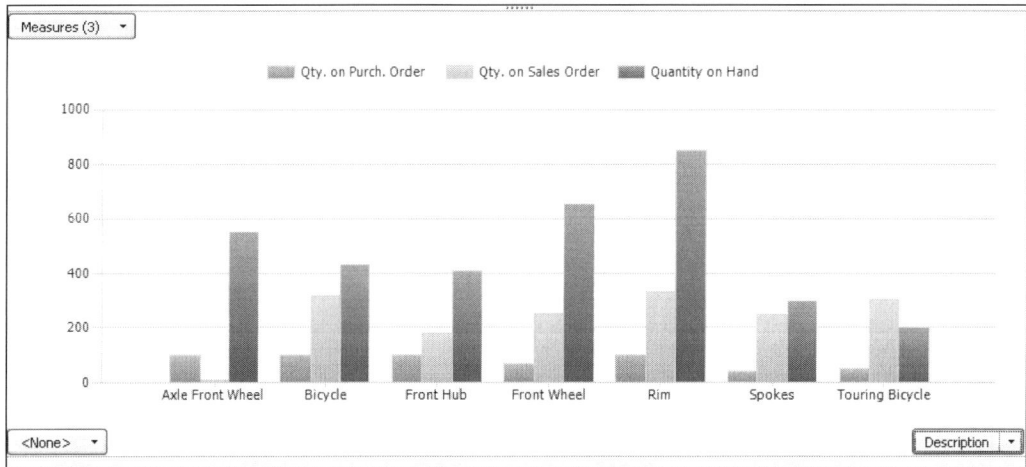

Creating charts for the Role Center home page

Another type of charts are the ones that are available in the Role Center for users to get quick analysis. The charts are predefined in the system and can be visible using the customize option in the Role Center.

In this section, we will see how to create custom charts and make them available on the home page:

1. To create a chart, open a text editor such as Notepad to write the XML code for the chart. In this example, we will design a chart for the number of customers per posting group.

2. Add the following XML code:

```xml
<?xml version="1.0" encoding="utf-8" ?>
<ChartDefinition xmlns:xsi=http://www.w3.org/2001/XMLSchema-instance                    xmlns:xsd="http://www.w3.org/2001/XMLSchema">
  <Title>
    <Text ID="ENU">Customers per CustomerPosting Group</Text>
    <Text ID="ENU">Customers per CustomerPosting Group</Text>
  </Title>
  <Table ID="18">
    <Filters>
```

```
        <Filter>
          <Field Name="No."/>
          <Value/>
        </Filter>
      </Filters>
    </Table>
    <XAxis ShowTitle="false">
      <Title/>
      <Field Name="Customer Posting Group"/>
      <Caption/>
    </XAxis>
    <YAxis>
      <Title/>
      <Measures>
        <Measure Operator="Count">
          <Caption>
            <Text ID="ENU">Count</Text>
            <Text ID="ENU">Count</Text>
          </Caption>
        </Measure>
      </Measures>
    </YAxis>
  </ChartDefinition>
```

3. Save the chart as a `<Name>.xml` file—for example `Test.XML`.

4. Once the chart is saved as an XML file, it has to be added to NAV. Open the Classic client and point to **Charts** under **Administration | Application Setup | RoleTailored Client**.

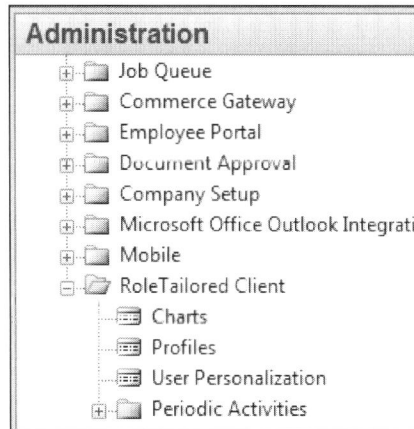

5. On the right-hand side, we can see the menu of charts available in the system:

ID	Name
18-02	Customers per Salesperson
270-01	Balances per Bank Account
272-01	Open Checks per Bank Account
36-01	SO per Currency
36-02	SO per Status
36-03	Sales Crdt Memos per Status
36-05	SO per Location
36-06	SO per Currency and Location
36-07	Sales Crdt Memos per Slsperson
36-08	SO per Date
37-01	SO Lines per Location
38-01	PO per Currency
38-02	PO per Status
38-03	Purch Credit Memos per Status
38-05	Open PO per Location
38-06	PO per Currency and Loc
38-07	Purch. C. Memo per Purchaser
18-02	Customers per Salesperson
18-03-A	Customers per Cust Posting Grp
270-01	Balances per Bank Account
5405-02	Prod. O per Status and WrkCnt
5406-01	Prod. O Lns Item Qty per Stat
5600-01	FA per FA Location and Subcl
5600-02	FA per FA Location

6. Select **Functions | Import Chart…**.

7. Point to the chart we just created in the earlier step. Once the chart is imported, start the RoleTailored client and customize page to add the newly added chart. The chart we just added should look like the following:

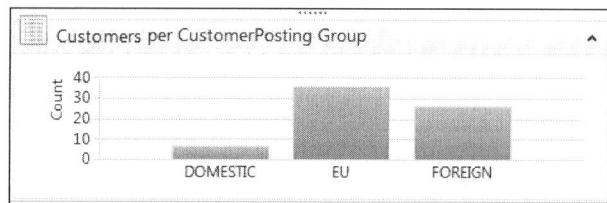

Reporting capabilities in NAV

Designing reports in NAV2009 is divided into the following parts:

- Defining the data model for the report
- Defining relationships
- Designing the layout
- Matrix design
- Adding links to external objects or other reports
- Conditional formatting

Defining the data model

The first step is to define the data model for the report. This is done using the Classic client option in NAV.

To define the data model, perform the following steps:

1. Open Object Designer from the Classic client by using the function key *F12* or from the **Tools** menu.

2. In Object Designer, click **Report** and then click the **New** button to open the new report.

3. In the **Table** field, click the drop-down arrow, and then select the table. In this example, we will design a report that shows the quantity of items sold to a customer. Therefore, choose the location table in the Table List window.

4. Select the **Create a Blank report** option. If we are designing a simple list or a form-type report, we can choose the **Create using Wizard** option. The wizard will guide us through the steps of choosing fields, which will automatically be placed on the report. In this example, we will design the layout using Visual Studio for the report to run using the RTC client, and hence we will go with the option of creating a blank report. Click on **OK**.

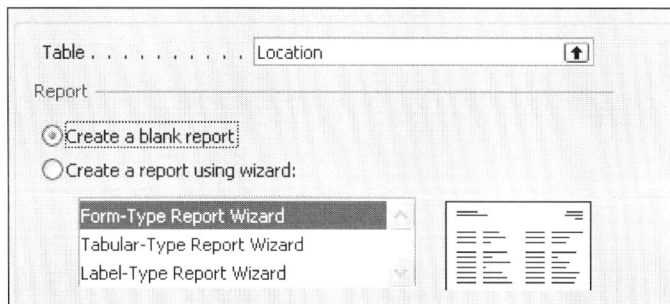

5. At this point, it is preferable to save the report and assign it an Object ID before designing it further. Close the report. Say **Yes** to the message for saving the report. The system will ask for an object ID and name for the report.

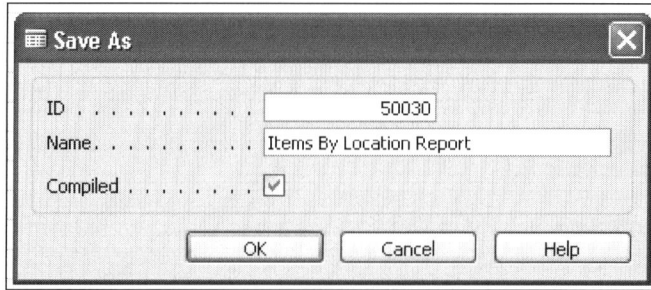

6. Assign an object ID and name for the report. This creates and saves the report.

7. Now go to the saved report by selecting the report from the list in the Object Designer and click on **Design**.

8. In the **Data Item** screen, select two tables in the two rows.

After the tables have been selected, we will now define relationships between these tables.

Defining relationships between tables

As we need to report on items sold by the customer, the items list should be grouped by customer.

1. Use the arrow buttons at the bottom-right of the screen to define levels of tables. The level for Item table should be 2. Use the right arrow button once to define this level for the Item table.

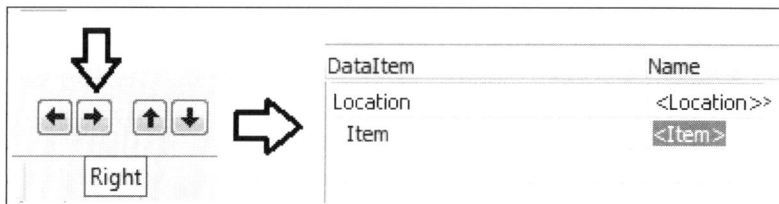

2. Pointing the cursor to a new line, select **Sections** from the **View** menu.

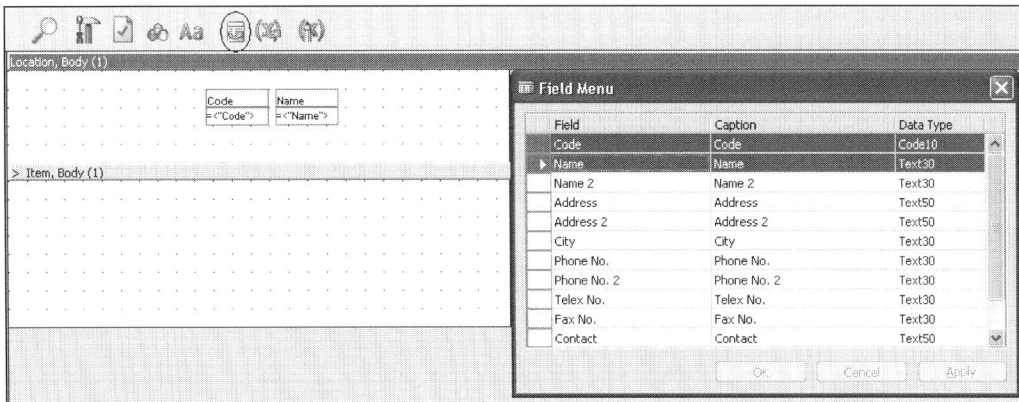

3. Use the **Field Menu** button to see the list of fields. Selecting the section **Location**, choose the fields `Code` and `Name` from the menu and drop them on the Customer section.

4. Similarly, add a few fields in the Item section. We will select the **Quantity on hand** and **No.** fields in this example.

5. Add a label control with the caption **Items by Location** on the top-left corner of the Location body.

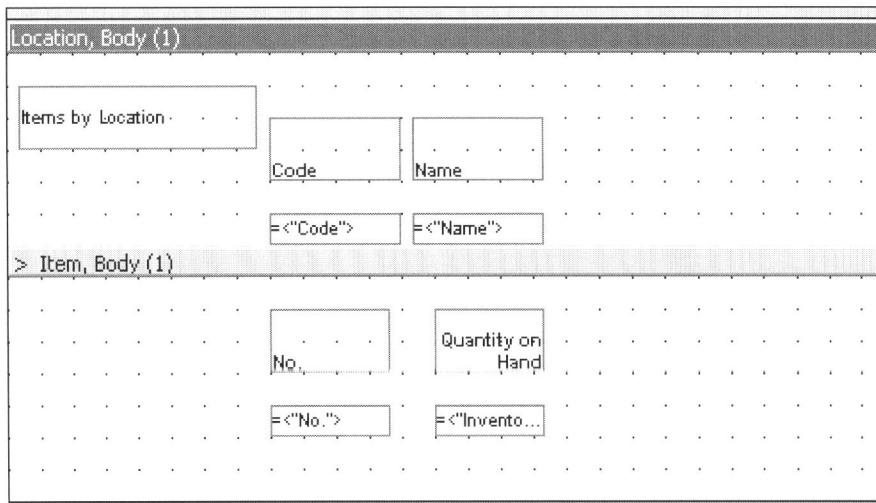

Defining the relationship between the tables

As we're using two tables in this report and need to report on a common field in the two tables, it's important to define the relationship between the two. To define the relationship, select the data item `Item`, open its properties and set the property `DataItemLink` to `Location Filter=FIELD(Code)`.

Property	Value
DataItemIndent	1
DataItemTable	Item
DataItemTableView	<Undefined>
DataItemLinkReference	<Location>
DataItemLink	<Undefined>| [...]
NewPagePerGroup	<No>
NewPagePerRecord	<No>
ReqFilterHeading	<>
ReqFilterHeadingML	<>
ReqFilterFields	<Undefined>
TotalFields	<Undefined>
GroupTotalFields	<Undefined>
CalcFields	<Undefined>
MaxIteration	<0>
DataItemVarName	<Item>
PrintOnlyIfDetail	<No>

Field	Reference Field
Location Filter	⬆ Code

Property	Value
DataItemIndent	
DataItemTable	Item
DataItemTableView	<Undefined>
DataItemLinkReference	<Location>
DataItemLink	Location Filter=FIELD(Code)
NewPagePerGroup	<No>
NewPagePerRecord	<No>
ReqFilterHeading	<>
ReqFilterHeadingML	<>
ReqFilterFields	<Undefined>
TotalFields	<Undefined>
GroupTotalFields	<Undefined>
CalcFields	<Undefined>
MaxIteration	

Now, as we have defined the data model and the relationships between the table, the next step is to define the layout.

Defining the layout

We need to do this in Visual Studio, which can be instantiated from the NAV report by clicking **Layout** in the **View** menu.

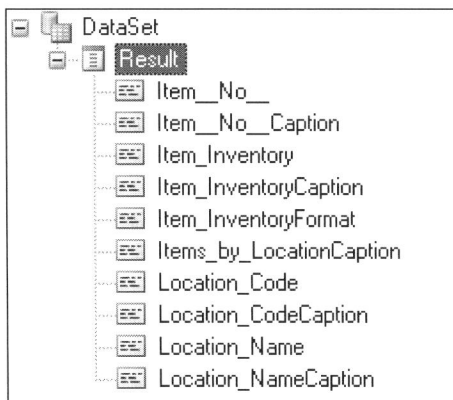

As shown in the preceding screenshot, the dataset in the report layout in Visual Studio should include all the fields and captions we defined in the classic design.

Selecting the matrix

We need to follow the steps given next to select the matrix:

1. Click on **Toolbox** and select a **Matrix** box for the layout.

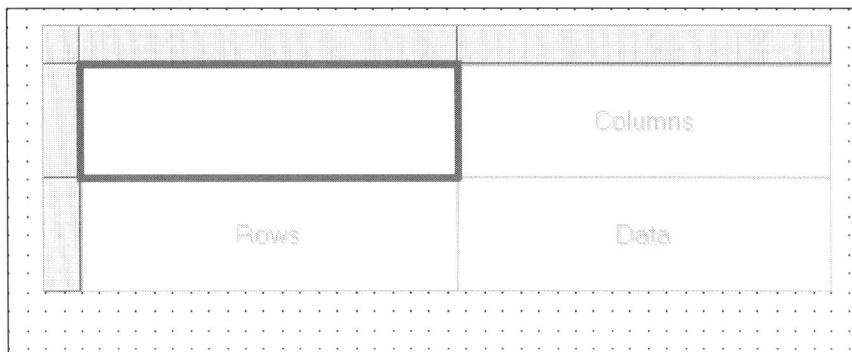

2. Place the **Items by Location** caption in the top-left cell of the matrix.

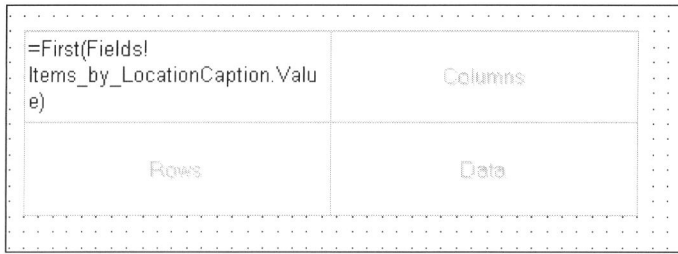

3. To insert a row, add a group in the Rows section of the layout. Right-click the Rows cell and click **Insert group**. In the expression area, select the `Item_No_.Value` field as shown in the following screenshot:

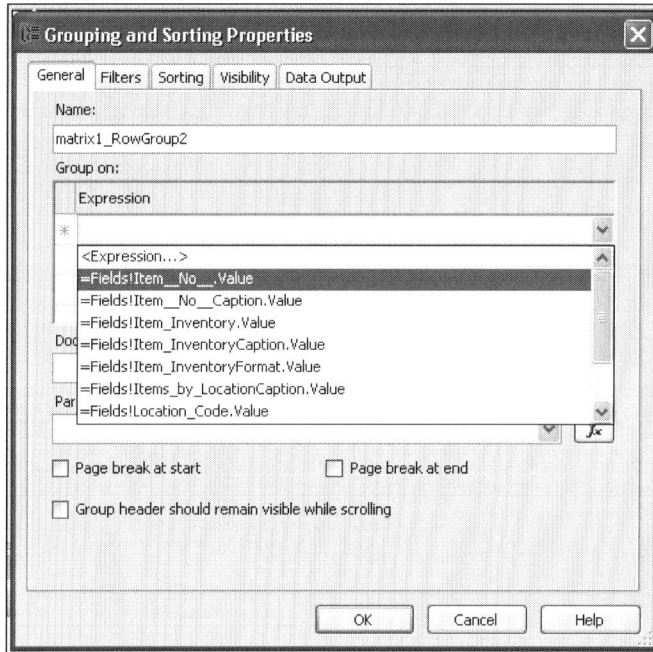

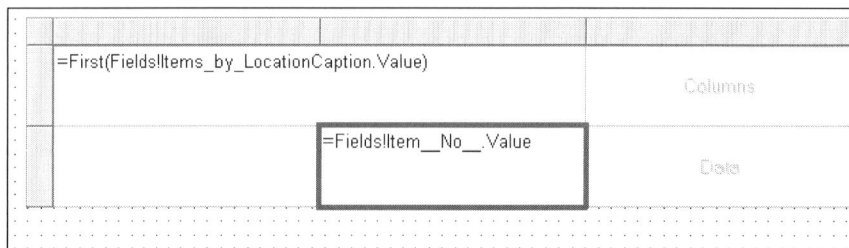

4. To add the Warehouse column above the data (No. of items), add `"=Fields!Location_Name.Value"` in the **Columns** area.

5. To add the data, drag the `Item_Inventory` field to the data area.

> The `Sum(Fields!Item_Inventory.Value)` is automatically added.

6. Add the columns in the cells by setting the `BorderStyle` property to **Solid**.

7. Our report should like the following screenshot:

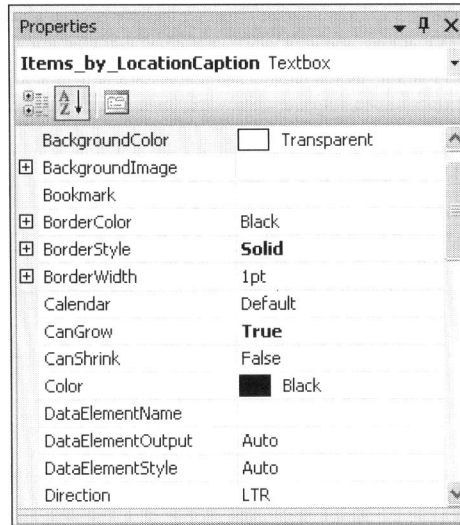

8. Save and close the report.

Testing the report

Now, as the report design is complete, the next step is to test the newly created report. We will start by saving the report first.

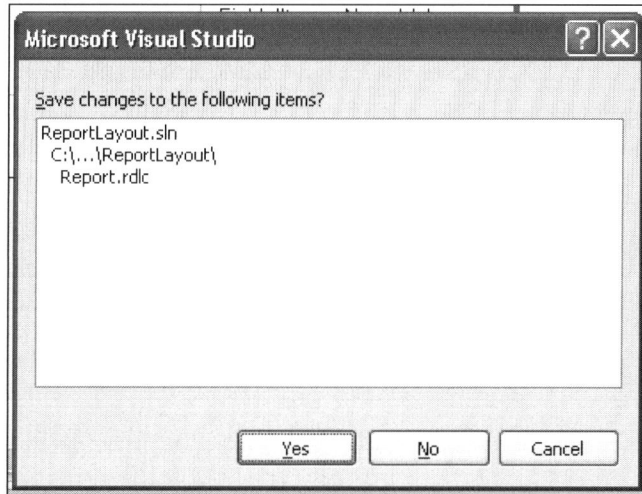

To test the report, we can add the report in the main page or can run it directly using the following command and parameters:

```
"dynamicsnav:// [machine name] /DynamicsNAV/ [company name] /
runreport?report=50030"
```

Consider the following example:

```
« dynamicsnav://localhost/DynamicsNAV/CRONUS International Ltd./
runreport?report=50030"
```

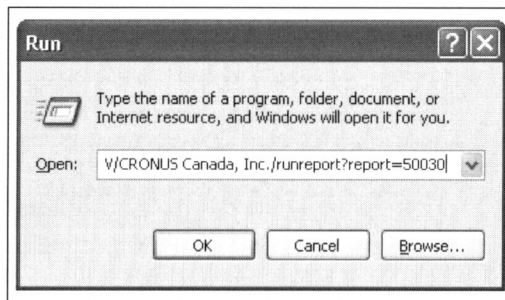

The report output should look like this:

Items by Location		Blue Warehouse	Green Warehouse	Outsourced Logistics
	0000001	0	0	0
	1000	432	432	432
	1001	200	200	200
	1100	652	652	652
	1110	850	850	850
	1120	300	300	300
	1150	410	410	410
	1151	550	550	550
	1155	200	200	200
	1160	200	200	200
	1170	200	200	200
	1200	152	152	152
	1250	200	200	200
	1251	10000	10000	10000
	1255	200	200	200
	1300	152	152	152
	1310	100	100	100

Dynamics NAV provides us with powerful tools and features to gain control and give us a crisp insight into our business. Future versions of NAV will see more Business Intelligence enhancements in the product such as stronger integration with SharePoint, PowerPivot integration, and more use of MS Office products with NAV.

Summary

In this chapter we learned about Business Intelligence, its categories, and product scenarios for each category. We also learned about the inherent BI capabilities in Dynamics NAV. Then we looked at creating charts for the Role Center homepage. Finally, we walked through steps for designing reports in NAV 2009 and testing them.

Index

lines type 48
list type 48
other requisites software, installing 51
setting up 48
users, setting up 55
Web Part Request templates, creating 54
enabled property 119
enhanced security model
about 70
and standard security model,
switching between 71
Enterprise Resource Planning (ERP) 5, 6
error messages
handling 96

F

find-as-you-type feature
disabling 116
FINDFIRST
used, for retrieving data 113, 114
FINDLAST
used, for retrieving data 113, 114
FINDSET
used, for retrieving data 113, 114
front end tab, Employee Portal
front end processing 53
reply queue 53
request queue 53

G

general tab, Employee Portal
code 52
description 52
use compression 52
use encryption 52
group 55

H

HotCopy backup
about 96
Dbtest parameter 97
description parameter 97
destination parameter 97
Nettype parameter 98
Osauthentication parameter 98

Password parameter 98
Servername parameter 98
source parameter 97
user parameter 98

I

Index Defrag tool 120-122
indexes/keys, Dynamics NAV
clustered property 120
enabled property 119
KeyGroups property 119
MaintainSIFTIndex property 120
MaintainSQLIndex property 119
SQLIndex property 120
SumIndexFields property 119
installing
Classic client 23-27
C/SIDE database server 28-35
Employee Portal 49, 50
Employee Portal frontend
components 51, 52
inter-company operability 15
ISEmpty 114

J

job queue
about 129
adjust exchange rates batch job 135
periodic jobs, examples 132
recurring journals 133
reminders batch job, creating 134
setting up 130-132

K

key exchange tab, Employee Portal
handle key exchange 53
key exchange reply queue 53
key exchange request queue 53
KeyGroups property 119
Key Information tool 123, 124

L

layout, NAV 2009 reports
defining 177

[PACKT] PUBLISHING enterprise
professional expertise distilled

Thank you for buying
Microsoft Dynamics NAV Administration

About Packt Publishing

Packt, pronounced 'packed', published its first book "Mastering phpMyAdmin for Effective MySQL Management" in April 2004 and subsequently continued to specialize in publishing highly focused books on specific technologies and solutions.

Our books and publications share the experiences of your fellow IT professionals in adapting and customizing today's systems, applications, and frameworks. Our solution based books give you the knowledge and power to customize the software and technologies you're using to get the job done. Packt books are more specific and less general than the IT books you have seen in the past. Our unique business model allows us to bring you more focused information, giving you more of what you need to know, and less of what you don't.

Packt is a modern, yet unique publishing company, which focuses on producing quality, cutting-edge books for communities of developers, administrators, and newbies alike. For more information, please visit our website: www.packtpub.com.

About Packt Enterprise

In 2010, Packt launched two new brands, Packt Enterprise and Packt Open Source, in order to continue its focus on specialization. This book is part of the Packt Enterprise brand, home to books published on enterprise software – software created by major vendors, including (but not limited to) IBM, Microsoft and Oracle, often for use in other corporations. Its titles will offer information relevant to a range of users of this software, including administrators, developers, architects, and end users.

Writing for Packt

We welcome all inquiries from people who are interested in authoring. Book proposals should be sent to author@packtpub.com. If your book idea is still at an early stage and you would like to discuss it first before writing a formal book proposal, contact us; one of our commissioning editors will get in touch with you.

We're not just looking for published authors; if you have strong technical skills but no writing experience, our experienced editors can help you develop a writing career, or simply get some additional reward for your expertise.

[PACKT] enterprise 🎛
PUBLISHING
professional expertise distilled

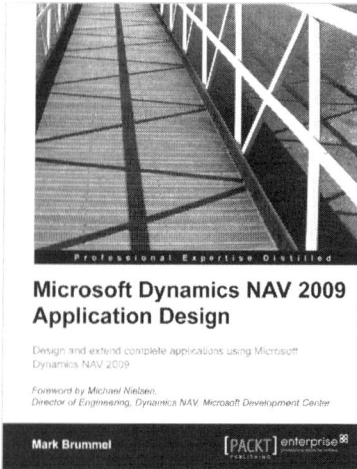

Microsoft Dynamics NAV 2009 Application Design

ISBN: 978-1-849680-96-7   Paperback: 496 pages

A focused tutorial for Microsoft Dynamics NAV application development

1. Learn how Dynamics NAV ERP suite is set up and customized for various industries

2. Integrate numerous parts of a company's operations including financial reporting, sales, order management, inventory, and forecasting

3. Develop complete applications and not just skeleton systems

4. Covers the design and implementation of two new add-on services: The Squash application and the Storage & Logistics application

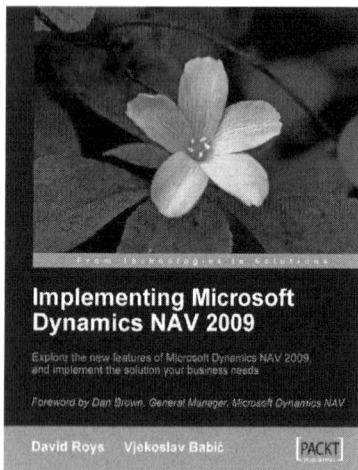

Implementing Microsoft Dynamics NAV 2009

ISBN: 978-1-847195-82-1   Paperback: 552 pages

Explore the new features of Microsoft Dynamics NAV 2009, and implement the solution your business needs

1. First book to show you how to implement Microsoft Dynamics NAV 2009 in your business

2. Meet the new features in Dynamics NAV 2009 that give your business the flexibility to adapt to new opportunities and growth

3. Easy-to-read style, packed with hard-won practical advice

Please check **www.PacktPub.com** for information on our titles

[PACKT] PUBLISHING enterprise
professional expertise distilled

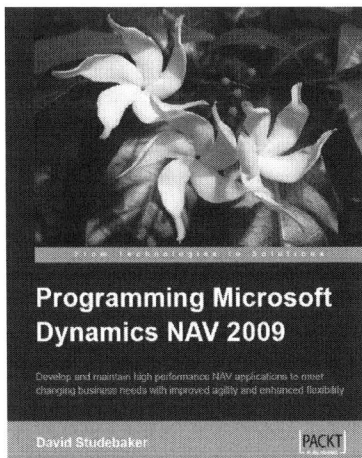

Programming Microsoft Dynamics NAV 2009

ISBN: 978-1-847196-52-1 Paperback: 620 pages

Develop and maintain high performance NAV applications to meet changing business needs with improved agility and enhanced flexibility

1. Create, modify, and maintain smart NAV applications to meet your client's business needs

2. Thoroughly covers the new features of NAV 2009, including Service Pack 1

3. Focused on development for the three-tier environment and the Role Tailored Client

4. For experienced programmers with little or no previous knowledge of NAV development

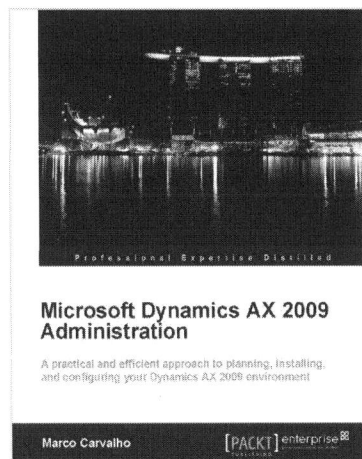

Microsoft Dynamics AX 2009 Administration

ISBN: 978-1-847197-84-9 Paperback: 328 pages

A practical and efficient approach to planning, installing and configuring your Dynamics AX 2009 environment

1. Effectively consolidate and standardize processes across your organization with a centralized source for a variety of business needs

2. Discover how to effectively plan and implement Dynamics AX 2009 in your business and fully grasp the necessary hardware, network, and software requirements to do so

Please check **www.PacktPub.com** for information on our titles

10764242R00116

Printed in Great Britain
by Amazon.co.uk, Ltd.,
Marston Gate.